TOOLS TO CHANGE THE WORLD

STUDY GUIDE BASED ON THE
PROGRESSIVE UTILIZATION THEORY (PROUT)
LEVEL 1

Dada Maheshvarananda and Mirra Price, M. Ed., Ed.M.

PROUTIST UNIVERSAL
COPENHAGEN

Proutist Universal
30 Platanvej, 1810 Fredriksberg
Copenhagen, Denmark

ACKNOWLEDGEMENTS

We would like to express our gratitude to the many people who have contributed to this Prout
Study Guide and to its predecessors. We especially want to thank Mark Friedman and Dada
Nabhaniilananda, whose work we have reprinted. We are grateful to all who offered suggestions on
the modules: Didi Ananda Devapriya (Romania), Ron Baseman, Ole Brekke and Kathrine Sumati
Brekke (Denmark), Alex Jackimovicz, Sid Jordan, Kathleen Kesson, John Linkart, Sloan McLain, Mal-
colm McDonell (Australia), Matt Oppenheim, Georgia Perry, Charles Paprocki, James Quilligan, and
Karl Robins. It has been extremely helpful that a few people—Howard Nemon, Didi Ananda Ruchira,
Nina Shapiro, and Bruce Dyer (New Zealand)—have conducted field test study groups and have given
feedback. Dada Maheshvarananda would also like to express his gratitude to the staff of the Prama
Institute and Wellness Center near Asheville, NC for allowing him to write in peace in their healing
environment. Dear readers, we also welcome your critical suggestions about how to improve this
project. Please write us at maheshvarananda@prout-global.org and mirra.price@prout-global.org.

Publisher's Cataloging-in-Publication data

Names: Maheshvarananda, Dada, author. | Price, Mirra, author.
Title: Tools to change the world : study guide based on the Progressive Utilization Theory (Prout) ,
level 1 / Dada Maheshvarananda and Mirra Price, M. Ed., Ed.M.
Description: Includes index. | Copenhagen, Denmark: Proutist Universal, 2018
Identifiers: ISBN 978-87-89552-00-2
Subjects: LCSH Prout (Economic theory) | Prout (Economic theory)--Study guides. | Sarkar, Pra-
bhat Ranjan, 1921-1990. | Economics--Philosophy. | Economics--Religious aspects. | Economics--So-
ciological aspects. | Economics--Moral and ethical aspects. | Monetary policy. | BISAC POLITICAL
SCIENCE / Public Policy / Economic Policy | POLITICAL SCIENCE / Political Ideologies / Commu-
nism, Post-Communism & Socialism | BUSINESS & ECONOMICS / Business Ethics
Classification: LCC HB72 .M233 2019 | DDC 330.12--dc23

Contents

FOREWORD

by James Quilligan

What Would Sarkar Do?

The Progressive Utilization Theory (Prout) was introduced in 1959 by Prabhat Ranjan Sarkar. In this visionary plan for social and economic management, Sarkar proposed that material goods be commonly owned and distributed fairly to meet everyone's basic needs. This would form the basis for an economy of producer and consumer cooperatives, small businesses, and key industries organized as public utilities.

Instead, in the decades that followed the launch of Prout, society has focused mainly on speeding up market growth. This became the leading worldview after the fall of Soviet communism in 1991. The mainstream belief is that global Gross Domestic Product (GDP) will continue to expand indefinitely through the production and use of materials and energy. In this self-generating system, personal initiative is the impetus behind a rising tide of wealth, while its benefits trickle down from the rich to the poor.

This structure has been challenged by recent circumstances, especially the Great Recession of 2008 and the austerity measures taken afterward. Many people now see that the availability of materials and energy — including arable land, water, fresh air, fossil fuels and rare earth minerals — is shrinking relative to the growing size and needs of the global population. Besides this decrease in non-renewable resources, a widening division between social classes and highly uncertain economic growth, there are the escalating financial costs and security risks posed by global climate change.

Our ideals of progress must be thoroughly reassessed .We must soon create a world that does not presently exist. This requires political action on a grand scale. It also means that unless this system-level transformation is carefully designed, global prosperity will devolve and humanity may not survive with any reasonable degree of safety or well-being.

Two major alternatives loom on the horizon. They could not be more different. One is a technology-driven corporate state which would undermine democracy and impose emergency management on global resources. Its leaders would appeal to popular fears in the name of restoring order and saving lives. The other course is the self-organization of production and distribution by the people themselves through participatory democracy. Put bluntly, the choice we face is between a centralized autocracy with increased competition for resources and a decentralized system of equality and cooperation for sustainable resources.

Sarkar's plan for democratic resource management is the only plausible solution. Through mutual planning and management in self-sufficient socioeconomic zones, communities could relocalize and human needs would be met more simply and ecologically. This is not a new idea. Projects for self-reliant ecodistricts are already operating in many areas — from traditional commons (rivers, forests, indigenous cultures, community restoration and bioregional governance) to emerging commons (solar energy, Internet, alternative currencies, urban co-ops and DGML programs for 'design global, manufacture local').

Yet these diverse practices are not woven together through an overarching set of policies. They lack a democratic political movement to bring them forward. As the world's economic crisis becomes more and more critical, we need a way to promote economic renewal in a free, fair and collaborative way. This requires an action plan based on universal knowledge and values that consciously touches the minds and hearts of everyone.

Breaking Through to a Post-Truth World

Like many organizations, Prout has not developed its message much beyond the standard flow model of knowledge: just present your information and assume people will act on it. This is the way that most of us were taught. It's also the culture of political discourse, media, and powerpoint presentations in which we've been raised. Likewise, many of us go to conferences and lectures, take in podcasts and webinars or read books and are exposed to a lot of information which we don't fully absorb or remember. Then program organizers wonder why their audiences are not more motivated by the topic at hand.

The reason is simple. Presenting information is only a first step toward personal and social transformation. Every audience requires some familiarity or prior experience with the knowledge, skills or attitudes that they are presented; otherwise, their beliefs and values will not be engaged and set into action. This crucial step is largely skipped by most presenters: *knowledge leads to new behavior only when it is combined with a change in personal attitude, interest or capacity.*

Nowhere has this created more confusion and misunderstanding than in conveying economic ideas. We witness how the news media attempts to be impartial by falsely comparing factual and non-factual sources of information. Yet we are less aware that a similar kind of imbalance exists in neo-classical economics. For example, the principle of supply and demand is celebrated for its scientifically balanced metrics; but the free market falsely equates the objective price of goods and the subjective needs of people. This makes us forget that economic demand is merely how much money we can pay for what we buy and does not measure the depth or extent of the needs that we cannot afford to satisfy.

As the blurring of fact and value becomes normalized, it creates an opening for social control through commercial and political propaganda. Citizens begin accepting these post-truth messages as real without checking whether opposing points of view are true. When values alone drive behavior and a behaviorist outlook dominates, our knowledge diminishes in importance. Gradually, we lose our standards for what comprises plausible information along with our basic reasoning skills for grasping policy options.

During the past hundred years, the psychology of behaviorism — the belief that people act solely through their bodily reflexes — has impacted every area of society, including education, economics and communication. Now, behaviorist politics have led to charges of 'fake news' against the media and other information sources. When fact-based knowledge informs our values, together they shape our behavior in healthy ways; but as values become detached from knowledge, our capacity to distinguish true from false is weakened. Without an informed attitude or educated interest, the relationship between personal behavior and values becomes inverted, leading us to act upon utterly false ideals. We may laugh when someone blurts, "Don't confuse me with the facts!" but it reveals a profound cultural cynicism and mistrust for the analytical way of processing information. Behaviorism not only reduces fact-based reality to a motor condition of the human brain, it denies the very existence of human consciousness.

Prout teaches that the neohumanistic integration of knowledge and values is a consciously spiritual activity. Nothing could be more important. Yet the Prout movement has not fully infused the psychology which this entails within its own messaging. Neither talking points nor talking heads can speak into people's deepest listening to dissolve the strong emotional grip of materialism. *Breaking through the illusions of a post-truth world requires that our presentations combine accurate information and principled values, leading our physical bodies to progressive action.* For this reason, the dynamic conjunction of factual knowledge and values-based ethics must be integrated within all our communications.

How Would Prout Do It?

Sixty years after PR Sarkar introduced his Progressive Utilization Theory, some fresh thinking has emerged on how to share the lessons of Prout in a more experiential way. In this manual, Dada Maheshvarananda and Mirra Price reject the notion that the linear imparting of knowledge will automatically cause people to adopt values or behavior. They acknowledge that a speaker can't just present one-way information and expect someone to suddenly endorse something as life-changing as economic transformation. Their collaborative work, *Tools to Change the World*, makes a significant contribution to the psychology of advocacy by showing how people's values, attitudes, worldviews, and orientations are also critical in changing their behavior.

Through simulations, games, group discussion, team learning, sensitivity training, group dynamics, and other forms of modeling, *Tools* challenges people to try on new personal behaviors. This readjusts the typical three-step communication flow — of introducing knowledge, developing values and shaping patterns of action — by ensuring that *human behavior integrates knowledge and values in unison.* So, as people take on new skill sets, experiences and new competencies, they are able to experience themselves more holistically and purposefully as they come across the economic concepts of Prout.

For that reason, *Tools* is not just for students. Along with its *Facilitator's Guide,* this book provides a way for teachers, trainers and changemakers to master the art of social transformation. In short, advocacy calls for strategic planning. *Before knowledge is introduced by a trainer, its developers must focus on both the purpose of the information and its expected depth of understanding by the public.*

With close study and application of this manual for economic change, the emerging global context for Prout comes more clearly into focus. As our deteriorating material and climactic conditions create a major financial crisis, it's likely that bloggers and politicians will continue spinning 'alternative facts' to justify a mad race for increasingly scarce resources. Yet, by presenting fact- and value-based economics in a way that allows people to organize themselves, *Tools* shows how society can develop balanced economic solutions by combining accurate knowledge with naturally arising beliefs. This is precisely how Prout's vital message will cut through the toxic air of post-truth perception, confusion and fear.

Restoring the dynamic balance between fact and value is the primary way of creating ethical and socially progressive behavior and comprehensive economic change. Embodying this creative tension is what turns trainees into activists and builds mass movements. *Tools* shows that this process is not the physical flow model of information > values > behavior. Rather, changes in individual behavior (such as action for cooperation and sustainability) must be preceded by one's emerging interests, attitudes or values (for social ownership and participatory control of resources), which in turn are rooted in self-reflective knowledge (like the ideas of Prout).

Unlike behaviorism, this is the conscious path of self-organization for individuals and societies alike. Dada Maheshvarananda and Mirra Price's brilliant handbook for creating economic democracy doesn't just speak this truth. It puts us in the position to live it.

James Quilligan has been an analyst and administrator in the field of international development since 1975. He has served as policy advisor and writer for many international politicians and leaders, including Pierre Trudeau, François Mitterrand, Edward Heath, Julius Nyerere, Olof Palme, Willy Brandt, Jimmy Carter and His Royal Highness Prince El Hassan of Jordan.

He was a policy advisor and press secretary for the Brandt Commission (1978-1984). He has been an economic consultant for government agencies in Mexico, Argentina, Ecuador, Brazil, Bolivia, Great Britain, the Netherlands, Belgium, France, Portugal, Germany, Austria, Norway, Denmark, Sweden, Ivory Coast, Algeria, Tanzania, Kuwait, India, Thailand, Indonesia, South Korea, Japan, Australia, Canada and the United States. In addition, Quilligan has served as an advisor for many United Nations programs and international organizations, including the International Monetary Fund.

He is presently Managing Director of Economic Democracy Advocates Foundation.

INTRODUCTION

Our two main goals for this course are to understand our world as it really is, and then to learn how to change it. There is power both in revealing the forces that control society from behind the scenes, and in sharing a vision of the world we really want and need.

The Progressive Utilization Theory (Prout) is a comprehensive socio-economic paradigm with a value base that includes basic principles; theories of history, society, and culture; political and economic systems; and a well-thought-out philosophy of ecology and social justice. Above all, it shares a vision for the future and a clear method to achieve social change.

Planet Earth needs impassioned activists working together to raise consciousness and change the world for the better. To do this we need to find creative solutions to severe problems in our rapidly changing environment.

This course presents problem-solving challenges and creative exercises designed to develop cooperative leadership skills.

Each module is designed to last a little more than two hours. This study guide can be used in at least six ways:

1. A group can meet weekly for two-and-a-half hour sessions for 10 weeks.
2. A group can meet for two intense weekends (10 hours each weekend).
3. It can be used as a five-day intensive training course.
4. It can be used as remote video conferencing for two-and-a-half hour sessions for 10 weeks with learners scattered in different locations (using a program like Zoom).
5. The content can be filmed to make an online distance learning course available for people to take at their convenience (with no discussion).
6. The manual can be read like a book (with no discussion).

The Background of the Study Circle

A study circle is a small group of people who meet to explore an issue or topic. Study circles began in the late nineteenth century as a democratic approach to self-education. Usually there is no teacher, but one member acts as facilitator to keep discussion flowing and on track. He or she also encourages participation and ensures that everyone has an opportunity to express themselves. In Sweden there are over 300,000 active study circles every year (Larsson and Nordvall 2010).

Those who care about the suffering in the world soon discover that social problems do not exist in isolation—they are deeply inter-connected and are part of a global system that is unjust. In the United States, civil rights and anti-war activists in the 1960s organized "macro-analysis" study circles to understand the roots of social and economic problems. At the end of that decade, women's consciousness-raising groups began forming. These women met to understand the roots and extent of sexism. They supported and empowered one another to overcome sexism in their personal lives and society (see Module 4).

An excellent online Study Guide was START (Study, Think, Act, Respond Together, 2007), which had its origins in the 1981 booklet *Organizing Macro-Analysis Seminars: Study & Action for a New Society* by the Philadelphia Macro-Analysis Collective of Movement.

It is vital to understand the big picture and to reveal the systemic nature of problems. At the same time, we need to focus on finding positive and effective actions that can be done locally.

Proutists have developed several guidebooks for Prout Study Circles.

1.) A Prout Study Guide, compiled by Ron Logan in 1976 with many short photocopies comparing Prout with different political, economic, spiritual, cultural, and other philosophies.

2.) A Women Proutists' Study Guide, compiled by Natalie Schaefer, Joanna Cazden, Andrea Carmen, Richard Gochal, and Satya Priya in 1979.

3.) A Comprehensive Guide to the Study of Prout by the Proutist Writers Group of New York Sector in 1998.

4) A Facilitator's Guide to the Universal Prout Study Circle Manual by Proutist Universal Maharlika (Philippines), in 2012.

5) *After Capitalism: Economic Democracy in Action* (InnerWorld Publications, 2012) by Dada Maheshvarananda and 13 contributing writers, assisted by over 70 people around the world. Some text and discussion questions from this book have been used in this study guide.

As you can see, this Prout Study Guide has had many contributors over more than four decades of evolution. *Tools to Change the World: Level 1* is simply the most recent version of an on-going process of study and dialogue. The world is constantly changing, as is the Prout movement. We hope that you find this current edition useful. We also hope you will join us, and provide insights and constructive feedback to this process of study and action.

Organizing a Study Circle

Some study groups fail because they are conducted poorly, with unfocused discussions and a few dominant voices. Other groups end after a few weeks because the participants are only studying; they're not *doing anything*. Rev. Martin Luther King, Jr. called this "paralysis of analysis," forever studying the issues and never acting. To avoid these problems, *Tools to Change the World: Level 1* is designed to be democratic, and to encourage real sharing. It inspires participants to start concrete work that will lead to a more just world society.

Group Size and Mix: We hope that everyone who likes this manual will feel confident enough to organize study circles. Invite friends, colleagues, and members of organizations you belong to. Use social media like Facebook and Meetup, and post flyers at strategic places in your neighborhood.

Generally, the best size for a study circle group is about 10. Ten members are enough to take on practical duties and to provide enough diversity to have good discussions. A group with fewer than eight members places an overly large burden on each person, especially if some people drop out over time. On the other hand, it is very difficult to have a discussion in too large of a group. With more than 17 people, it is best to split into two separate groups.

This study guide is geared toward adults. Some high school students are mature enough to engage with these concepts and ideas, but younger people typically are not.

How Much Time for Each Module? Most groups meet once a week. This works well and helps the group maintain focus and momentum. A group focused more intensely on study, such as a college class, might meet twice a week. Other groups, with members who have many other commitments, might decide to meet less often. However, we recommend that you meet at least twice a month so that the group maintains cohesion and members do not lose track of ideas from earlier sessions.

We realize that sessions shorter than two-and-a-half hours may work better for some people and that longer sessions may be tiring. However, anything less than two-and-a-half hours will make the group feel rushed, will reduce the quantity and quality of discussion, and will make the exercises impractical. We encourage groups to have a short break in longer sessions.

Meeting Place: A good meeting place is one that is easy to find and travel to, and large enough with enough chairs for everyone. It should also be private and quiet, so members can speak freely and without distraction.

Set the chairs up in a rough circle so everyone can see one another. Have a large easel (or a chair and a board set up as an easel), blackboard, whiteboard, or a blank wall where the group can record notes on large pieces of paper ("wall charts"). Or you can use a laptop computer and a projector.

The living room in a private home, or a meeting room at a library, church, community center, or labor hall are all good places. Restaurants, bars, and social clubs are usually noisy and distracting. If you meet at a member's home, you may want to change to a different house each session so that no one person is burdened by hosting the group repeatedly.

Punctuality: Start each session on time and end on time. If people come late, they will miss out. The initial activities of each module are designed to function well even if some members have not yet arrived. Don't punish those who arrive on time by forcing them to wait for latecomers. Close on time, too, so that participants can get to their next appointments on time.

Expectations: Study circles work well when participants commit to the process and to the other members. Each person should agree to:

Try their best to attend all ten sessions for the full time (two-and-a-half hours each).

Read the assigned module before each session.

Participate honestly in discussions and exercises.

Work with others cooperatively.

Sometimes accept an additional role as facilitator, timekeeper, etc.

Do as many additional readings and viewings as possible.

Do as many activities as possible.

Deliver good, succinct presentations to the group.

Despite people's best intentions, events sometimes prevent them from fulfilling all their commitments. Still, *Tools to Change the World* is important. By committing to this challenge to learn and use these tools, the course stays relevant, interesting, inspiring, and fun.

In Which Country and Year Do You Live? Both the authors of this Study Guide are in the United States, so most of the examples and supporting statistics are from there. We used the most current data we could find in 2018. We strongly encourage facilitators to look up relevant current data in each module from your region and country.

The Design of Each Module

Excitement Sharing (in Facilitation Guide): "What is something good that has happened in your life since we last met? Or would anyone like to read from your journal or share your recent activities?" The first module explains journaling as an activist tool. Indirectly, it encourages note-taking. More importantly, it causes everyone to reflect on the ideas and tools of the course outside of the meetings.

Everyone does not have to say something in Excitement Sharing every week. This section should be limited to 5-10 minutes.

The Social Reality: This is a short five-minute presentation about a particular social problem in our world, such as poverty, hunger, unemployment, debt, corruption, pollution and climate change, etc. Rather than just reading this text to the group members, all of whom have hopefully already read it, the facilitator should tell it in his or her own words. Ideally this would include relevant statistics for the country and community where the study circle is meeting.

The Social Reality Discussion Question (in Facilitation Guide): Then each person takes a minute to express how the problem directly or indirectly impacts her or him. The facilitator concludes by saying, "Excuse me, please, but we're going to end this discussion now because, as usual in this course, we want to focus on the solutions." (10 minutes).

Cooperative Game (in Facilitation Guide): These are team-building exercises that create powerful, safe learning experiences. Cooperative games help participants interact and share, gain self confidence, improve collaboration, and develop genuine compassion for others. As Bill Ayers said, these are "cooperative calisthenics, little exercises to prepare us for the huge changes that are essential to our survival on this earth" (Maheshvarananda 2017, 1). (Bill Ayers is a social justice organizer and activist, a teacher and former Distinguished Professor of Education at the University of Illinois at Chicago; in the 1960s he co-founded the radical Weather Underground.) (10-15 minutes).

Prout's Vision: The analysis and vision of Prout are powerful tools for changing the world. Social problems are inter-connected and caused by an exploitative global economic system. The fundamentals of Prout help us understand the root causes of social and economic problems. Prout's vision for a better way to organize the economy, government, medicine, agriculture, education, the workplace, and other fields clarifies not only what we're against, but even more importantly, what we stand for. (20 minutes).

Discussion Questions (in Facilitation Guide): After the presentation, the group can discuss some of the questions. There is no need to discuss them all—different people will find some questions more interesting than others. The facilitator can also ask different questions. There are no right or wrong answers. The questions prompt participants to think about the ideas in the module, and so each reply will be, by definition, their honest opinion. One way to do this is to go around the group, allowing each person a chance to answer, and starting with a different person each time. Explain that anyone can pass if they want more time to think, and also can give their opinion at the end if they think of something later. Only after everyone has answered, will people be allowed to speak again.

Activist Tools: "Philosophers have only interpreted the world, in various ways. The point, however, is to change it." - Karl Marx. The twelve activist tools included in this manual are proven techniques that unlock our capacity to educate, to build collective power and to make change. Grassroots community organizing skills are mighty arms, even when the wealthy and powerful oppose us. Learning and practicing these activist tools empower us to do something concrete.

Activist Tool Exercise (in Facilitation Guide): The activist skills include an exercise to practice using the tool together.

Self Reflection (in Facilitation Guide): At the end of each module, the facilitator answers the question, "How do you feel you did?" After answering, he or she has the option of asking the other members to also give constructive feedback.

Written Feedback (in Facilitation Guide): Written anonymous feedback forms are also very helpful. Ask participants to fill them out on the spot before they leave, while the experience is still fresh in their minds.

Activities: There are further activities, some of which involve community research projects, showing how the Prout Vision applies to your situation. The more activities that you do, alone or in groups, the more engaged you will become.

Further Readings and Viewings: These are articles and videos freely available on the Internet that participants can access in order to further their learning experience.

Democratic Group Process

The Progressive Utilization Theory is comprehensive, addressing politics, economics, culture, history, psychology, and much more. Its founder, Prabhat Ranjan Sarkar, dictated approximately 1,500 pages on Prout. Because of the breadth of the material, few people feel confident to teach it. Many people have learned a little and like what they find, yet always look for an experienced Proutist to lead any discussion about Prout. If none is available, Prout discussions do not take place.

To overcome this difficulty, *Tools to Change the World* is designed to empower anyone to start a democratic study group. As the great Brazilian revolutionary educator Paulo Freire insisted, we all have different kinds of knowledge, so by sharing, we will always learn.

To keep the group on track while preventing anyone from dominating the discussion or decision-making, the participants should take on the following roles in rotation:

Convener and Host: This is the one who starts the Study Circle and recruits participants. They arrange the logistics of the first meeting, arrange child care, welcome everyone when they arrive, and usually facilitate that first meeting to show the group how it's done. Afterwards the role of host can also rotate.

Facilitator: Each week a different participant will be encouraged to prepare and present, in his or her own words, the material for the following module. The facilitator should:

Plan: With the assistant facilitator, develop a meeting agenda. Set time limits for each item, based on this study guide, the desires of the group, and feedback from the previous meeting. Before the meeting, display the agenda with time limits on a large wall chart in the meeting room.

Start and end the meeting on time.

Apply Agreements: At the beginning of the meeting, review the agenda and time limits with the group. Make any changes the group desires and agrees on together. Throughout the meeting, keep the group on task. Suggest when it is appropriate to move on to the next agenda item. If the group expresses a desire to change the agenda, help the group make a new agreement, and then enforce it.

Guide: Introduce each agenda item or ask someone else to do so. Remind the group when they have strayed from the agenda, perhaps by asking if they want to return. Keep reports, discussion, and brainstorming sessions within agreed-upon time limits.

Encourage: Help everyone share in the discussion. Be sensitive to reserved people being cut off or intimidated by more outgoing folks. Encourage those who have not participated much to speak more and encourage those who talk a lot to listen more and speak less. Help the other members of the group who have taken on roles to do their jobs.

Monitor: Be sensitive to the feelings of the group members. Note expressions of emotion or uneasiness, which may indicate that some change in the process is needed.

Reveal: Try to get important but unspoken frustrations, needs, fears, expectations, etc., out in the open so they can be dealt with directly and with respect. "Hidden agendas" are often an important source of failure and frustration in groups.

Summarize at times what has been said including disagreements, and ask the group, "Is that accurate?" This reassures people that they have been heard.

Sort: Suggest ways to separate unlike ideas and group together similar ideas. Point out agreements and disagreements.

Synthesize: Suggest ways that solutions or ideas can be melded together. Different approaches may reinforce one another.

Suggest Directions: Focus the discussion by suggesting a particular order. Begin with one item, and then proceed to others.

Mediate: When people seem unable to hear each other, ask them to repeat in their own words what they think they heard. Then ask if the speaker felt it was an accurate re-statement of what they meant. If not, invite the person to rephrase the idea until everyone understands.

Assistant Facilitator: This person assists the facilitator in all duties and is the backup if the facilitator is unable to come. Typically, the assistant facilitator will become facilitator for the next module.

Timekeeper: This is a crucial, yet delicate role. No one likes to be interrupted when they are speaking. When an engaging discussion or an exciting activity is underway, participants will naturally want to continue. The timekeeper should give people a minute or two of warning, mainly during reports, so that they can use the rest of their time wisely. The role of the timekeeper is to gently remind the speaker or the group when the allotted time is over, and to ask if the group wants an extension. If the consensus is yes, the timekeeper should either suggest ten more minutes or ask the group how much longer they want to spend on this discussion.

Recorder: This person writes notes on the wall chart when it is useful to the group. This may include recording agenda changes, important facts or ideas mentioned in reports, brainstormed ideas for action, ideas proposed in the evaluation section, etc. Despite the best efforts of the recorder, it is sometimes difficult to recognize important ideas that should be recorded as they come up. So it is useful to have a separate piece of paper posted to the side where anyone can record thoughts if she or he feels the need.

References

Larsson, Staffan and Henrik Nordvall. 2010. "Study Circles in Sweden: An Overview with a Bibliography of International Literature." Linköping: Linköping University Electronic Press.

Maheshvarananda, Dada. 2017. *Cooperative Games for a Cooperative World: Facilitating Trust, Communication and Spiritual Connection*. Puerto Rico: Innerworld Publications.

MODULE 1: THE RIGHT TO LIVE

Check Your Understanding

At the end of this module, you should be able to explain the following concepts:

What is extreme poverty and relative poverty?

What are the five minimum necessities of life?

What should be the first priority of an economy?

What role, if any, should the government have in helping citizens find meaningful employment with fair wages?

How does Prout measure economic advancement?

What should be done with surplus wealth?

What are the strengths and weaknesses of Karl Marx's ideas?

What are the three elements of a good story?

Why is it important to tell your personal story?

What are three benefits of journaling?

The Social Reality: Poverty

Poverty is defined differently by different organizations. The United Nations defines extreme poverty as people living on $1.25 or less per day, and calculates that 1.2 billion people in the world suffered extreme poverty in 2015, one out of every six people (UNDP 2014). According to UNICEF, poverty kills more than 15,000 children each day (UNICEF 2017).

In addition, each country determines "relative poverty," a standard of living at which one cannot purchase the basic necessities in that society. For example, the 2018 poverty level in the United States is $12,140 per year for a single individual, or $33 per day (HHS 2018). According to the Census Bureau, 40.6 million Americans, or 12.7 percent of the population, are at that level (Semega, Fontenot, and Kollar 2017). On any given night, over 550,000 people in the United States experience homelessness (HUD Exchange 2017). Nine percent of Americans have no health care insurance and many more have only limited coverage, causing millions to fall into poverty when their family is hit by a medical emergency (Barnett and Berchick 2017). And 43 million Americans are receiving food stamps (Kutner 2018). All this in one of the richest countries of the world.

Around the world, women and children, refugees, and all oppressed peoples suffer poverty in much greater proportions than the rest of the population. The majority of the world's poor are women, because they are lower-paid, unpaid, and undervalued. Globally, women earn 23 percent less than men. At the current rate of progress, it will take 170 years to close the gap. Seven hundred million fewer women than men are in paid work (OXFAM 2018).

Prout's Vision: Guarantee the Minimum Necessities of Life to All

It is important to understand that poverty is completely unnecessary. In his book, *The End of Poverty*, Jeffrey Sachs made some careful estimates about the cost to end extreme poverty. To end extreme poverty worldwide in 20 years, the total cost per year would be about $175 billion (Munk 2013). This represents only ten percent of the $1.7 trillion that the world spends on military and arms (Musaddique 2017). The world has enough resources to end poverty everywhere. Unfortunately, that is not one of the goals of global capitalism.

The Progressive Utilization Theory or Prout asserts that guaranteeing the right to live for everyone has to be the first priority of every country. "The minimum necessities of all should be guaranteed in any particular age" (Sarkar 1992, 4).

Prout recognizes five basic necessities of life: food (including pure drinking water), clothing, housing (including sanitation and energy), medical care, and education. Other requirements are local transportation and communication. This birthright transcends citizenship—meaning that every human being, whether native or visitor to a country, must be guaranteed these necessities.

Providing the basic necessities should be the primary function and duty of any economy. Human beings require these in order to realize their true human potential, to develop culturally, and to achieve inner fulfillment. Without necessities, the "pursuit of happiness" remains beyond the reach of the world's poor.

Most governments provide a safety net to help ensure that the poor and most vulnerable do not fall below a minimally accepted level of poverty and destitution. Unfortunately, except for Scandinavian countries, most government safety nets provide a very low bar that prevents only the worst suffering. Millions of citizens worldwide face great hardship with insufficient housing, health care, and food.

The right to have meaningful employment with fair wages is also a basic human right. Rather than relying on hand-outs from government agencies (as in the welfare systems of liberal democratic countries), people need jobs. It is the responsibility of all levels of government to foster full employment, with jobs that utilize each worker's skills and capabilities.

A just minimum wage, often called a "living wage," must be set high enough so that people can buy the necessities. At present, in many countries, there is neither a guarantee of work nor a living wage. Without the guarantee of a living wage, work loses its appeal; without jobs, the promise of good wages is empty. Guarantees of work and a living wage go together.

Some welfare systems actually motivate people not to work. In the United States, for example, those who receive welfare must immediately report any dollar they earn, which is usually deducted from their next welfare check. They are not allowed to borrow money to start a small business without immediately sacrificing their monthly assistance. In this way, welfare recipients sometimes become emotionally dependent, prisoners of both poverty and the welfare system which seeks to alleviate it. Thus a whole class of people who should be employed remains jobless, or becomes part of the underground informal economy.

Prout, on the other hand, by guaranteeing jobs that provide a livable minimum wage, would limit welfare as a special contingency for those who are physically or mentally unable to work. Efforts will be made to find appropriate jobs for people with all types of disabilities, so that they, too, can feel fulfillment that they are earning a living wage and contributing to society.

Deciding what are the minimum necessities must be done in a realistic and progressive way; there must be continual adjustment of the basic requirements, depending upon available resources and local standards. Standards for minimum necessities will change with time and place.

For example, staple foods are different in different cultures, yet they must all meet adequate nutritional standards. Clothing varies according to climate and culture. Minimum housing standards appropriate to the local climate and culture must also be determined. The availability of better housing is an incentive to be built into the system. Everyone, however, will be guaranteed a roof over their head, regardless of their social standing.

We are describing a post-capitalist Prout economy, where increasing profits and lowering costs and wages are not the goal. Improving the quality of life for every human being is our goal. In the following modules, we will learn more about how checks and safeguards will ensure that this happens.

In a Proutist framework, the people's **purchasing capacity** will be taken as the measure of economic progress. A number of factors are required to increase purchasing capacity. These include basic goods and services, stable prices, appropriate wage increases, and increasing collective wealth and productivity.

Imagine a world in which no one need worry about getting enough money to buy food, clothes, housing, education, and medical care for his or her family!

Rational Incentives

"The surplus wealth should be distributed among meritorious people according to the degree of their merit" (Sarkar 1992, 5).

This surplus is known in Proutist economics by the Sanskrit word, *atiriktam*', and addresses the problems of equal distribution found in communist approaches. It is used as an incentive to motivate people to give greater service to society. Atiriktam' can, for instance, be given as increased salary or as other benefits. Its purpose is to encourage people to develop their skills and increase their capacity to assist society. Atiriktam' can take the form of task-related privileges. For example, a talented researcher may be given access to expensive laboratory facilities, while an effective and selfless social worker may be offered more support staff.

In an article published shortly before his death in 1990, entitled "Minimum Requirements and Maximum Amenities," Sarkar expanded on the relationship between minimum salary and atiriktam'. He stressed that while providing the minimum necessities, people should not be left with a bare-bones existence. Higher salaries should be provided to the meritorious, yet continuous and collective effort will be needed to raise the economic standard of the common people to an appropriate level for that time and place (Sarkar 1992, 58).

Karl Marx and his Marxist and Communist Legacy

Karl Marx (1818–1883) was a German economist, historian, and political philosopher whose theories revolutionized the world. He wrote a brilliant three-volume analysis of capitalism, *Das Kapital*, which is approximately 3,000 pages long. He showed that capitalism, by its very nature, inevitably exploits people. Its excesses, contradictions, and weaknesses contribute to its decay. Marx's compassion for the oppressed and his compelling call to end exploitation are the hallmarks of his work.

His theories are taught around the world. All Marxists believe that the minimum necessities of life should be guaranteed to all. Marxists have led many of the social and economic advances in this direction over the last hundred years. The founder of Prout, P.R. Sarkar, respected Marx, saying he was "a good person, a thoughtful person, and a prophet for the poor" (Devashish 2010).

However, Marx was not very clear about what should replace capitalism. He called for "an association of free men, working with the means of production held in common, and expending their many different forms of labor power in full self-awareness as one single social labor force" (Marx 1887). That vague statement, along with a few others, is all we have to define Marx's economic alternative.

There are also internal inconsistencies in his work. For example, Marx's "labor theory of value" stated that the value of an object equals the cost of the labor required to produce or extract it. But in the 21st century, we have become painfully aware that all natural resources are limited, and many are non-renewable. Scarcity increases value. Each natural resource has an intrinsic and constantly increasing value and should be utilized in the best way possible.

The Marxist axiom, "from each according to his ability, to each according to his need," sounds good in theory. However, most people need some incentive to motivate them. To distribute surplus wealth equally is not reasonable. "Diversity, not identity, is the law of nature... Those who want to make everything equal are sure to fail because they are going against the innate characteristic of [nature]" (Sarkar 1992). Leaders who tried to apply Marx's ideas in different countries faced many practical problems, because incentives are an important factor in economics.

Marx spoke of the "materialist conception of history," and later his colleague Friedrich Engels and others coined the term "dialectical materialism" to describe the Marxist perspective. Materialism holds that the only thing that exists is matter, and everything, including consciousness, is the result of material interactions. The Russian Soviet leader Vladimir Lenin repeated throughout his life that "the concrete analysis of the concrete situation" was the very soul of Marxism (Burlatsky 1963).

The problem is that when all spiritual experience is denied, people's mental longings focus on material pleasures. When one always thinks on material reality, the mind becomes materialistic and the baser instincts are aroused. Sarkar, on the other hand, emphasized: "as you think, so you become." By thinking noble and uplifting thoughts, we become better people.

Like Marx, Sarkar promoted social equality, calling Prout "progressive socialism"(Sarkar 1988). Prout advocates public or common ownership and cooperative management of the means of production and the allocation of resources, which is a common definition of socialism. Yet it differs markedly from Marxism in many ways. (Marx's class analysis is compared with Prout's in Module 9.)

Marx and Engels published *The Communist Manifesto* in 1848, calling for a revolutionary Communist Party to lead the working class in revolt against capitalist exploitation. It reviewed the history of class struggle and the problems of capitalism, but said very little about how Communist Parties should rule.

In fact, communist governments have frequently alienated most of their people (Tong 1995). Fifty years after leading the communist revolution in Cuba, Fidel Castro was asked if their economic system was still worth exporting to other countries. He replied, "The Cuban model doesn't even work for us anymore" (Goldberg 2010).

In centralizing both political and economic power in the hands of the state, many communist leaders fell victim to a shortsighted belief that they could not fail. This arrogance, combined with a materialist philosophy and the belief that the ends justified the means, has resulted in Communist Party tyranny.

Communist regimes throughout the world have oppressed their own people. Political repression, imprisonment, forced labor camps, executions, and famines caused by the forced takeovers of land and centralized economic policies, were the worst crimes. The estimated combined death toll in Stalin's Soviet Union, Mao's China, and Pol Pot's Cambodia range from 21 million to 70 million (Valentino 2005).

Communist Party dictators have ordered their military to imprison or kill people if they tried to protest or escape. They censored artistic expression, banned private enterprise, stifled personal initiative, and prohibited religious and spiritual freedom. In Eastern Europe and Russia, their own people have overthrown these dictatorships in popular revolts. However, five nations are still controlled by communist parties: China, Cuba, Vietnam, Laos, and North Korea.

Prout rejects indiscriminate violence and terrorism. The Proutist approach is to change consciousness through mass education, inspiration, and a cultural renaissance—not through fear. Political revolution can never create a just society unless the tendency to exploit others is overcome in the minds of the leaders and people.

Sarkar wrote, "The concepts of dialectical materialism, the materialist conception of history, the withering away of the state, proletariat dictatorship, classless society, etc., are defective ideas which can never be implemented. That is why the post-revolutionary stage in every communist country has suffered from turmoil and oppression" (Sarkar 1969).

Activist Tools: Narratives: Telling your Story

Some of this material is taken from the successful climate change organization, 350.org.

We all dream of telling our stories, of expressing what we think, feel, and see before we die. Everyone has a compelling story that can move others. But few people know how to do this well. We've all heard people talk on and on, telling irrelevant details, leaving us bored instead of inspired. Have you ever listened to a story like that?

This is *not* okay. Because you have a story to tell, and it must be told well.

Influential individuals and organizations tell a story that is so compelling others can't help but want to join it. Listeners should feel "Me, too!" Telling your story is an essential recruiting tool for community organizers and movement builders.

You need to practice. You need to become an expert at telling your own story. Consider some of the basic elements of any good story and how they apply to your story:

What's the conflict?

Who's the hero?

Where is the suspense?

How will the conflict resolve?

What's the point?

Why does it matter?

Classic stories, myths, and fairy tales follow this archetype. The conflict gets worse and the protagonist experiences a major problem at some point—all seems lost before it gets better and redemption happens. Apply these same elements to your own tale.

Telling your story helps you make sense of your life—why certain events happened the way they did. You can see what has happened to you and through you. You begin to make sense of who you are. Telling your story can be healing, and the practice leads to greater confidence and understanding.

In this workshop we will not only learn how to tell our story, we will also learn how to coach others to tell a good story.

Story-Telling Key: values inspire action through emotion. We must learn how to engage both the head and the heart to inspire people to act.

Much of the news makes people feel alienated, helpless, and afraid. Inertia, fear, self-doubt, isolation, and apathy paralyze people. Have you ever felt that way?

To overcome these negative feelings, we need to inspire people with positive emotions that urge us to take action: urgency, hope, solidarity, righteous anger, and YCMAD, which stands for "You can make a difference!" The stories that we learn to tell will stir emotions that urge people to take action and to overcome emotions that keep them from action.

"Hook": A hook is your opening line, an attention-getter, the question or quote that immediately hooks your listener. The more off-the-wall or mysterious, the better. Dare your audience to get excited.

Three Elements of a Story

Introduction – The Challenge: Perhaps your challenge was to climb a mountain, or perhaps it was a deep hole like addiction that you managed to climb out of. Overcoming traumas inspires us. What was so hard about this challenge? Why was it your challenge?

The Choice: Why did you make the choice you did? Where did you get the courage (or not)? Where did you find the hope (or not)? How did it feel?

Conclusion – The Outcome: How did the outcome feel? Why did it feel that way? What did it teach you? What do you want it to teach us? How do you want us to feel?

Activist Tools: Journaling

To be an effective activist, to change the world, we must awaken our consciousness and consider many radical ideas and perspectives. This course is designed to challenge you at every step, so it is natural that you will experience profound emotions, too.

Journaling is a powerful way to track your personal journey of head and heart. How do you feel about each new idea you encounter? Each story you hear? Each cooperative activity? Each action?

Journaling can help you overcome your fears and spur personal growth. Journaling is just the writing down of your thoughts and feelings at any given moment in as much detail, and with as little inhibition or censorship as possible. This is sometimes called "free writing," "automatic writing," or "stream-of-consciousness" writing. It's less about detailing the events in your life, and more about your thoughts, and especially your feelings, surrounding them.

Many of history's most famous revolutionaries, scholars, and scientists, among others, kept a journal or maintained extensive self-reflective correspondence, considering it to be an essential part of their quest to lead a meaningful life. You should, too. Journaling may, in fact, be the single most efficient route to the Socratic goal: to live an examined life.

In *Writing Down the Bones*, Natalie Goldberg suggests to set aside at least 30 minutes a day for writing. Setting a timer is helpful. If you are upset or angry, write like a demon. Your sentences may be short. (Your journal is a window into your emotional state.) After this half hour, sometimes called The Journaling Arc, you will probably feel calmer and more focused, and maybe you will feel more compassion, too, toward the concerning people and situation. If you observe The Journaling Arc in your journal entries, you can use it to track your emotional growth throughout your activism and life.

When the time is up, you can either stop writing or continue. In this way, you can start a positive habit of setting down your thoughts and feelings every day. Goldberg suggests not being afraid to lose control, and to keep the hand moving (Goldberg 1986).

The goal is to move past our internal censors and get to a place of writing what we actually see and feel, not what we think we should see and feel. Especially, when we first start writing, we may feel swept away by our emotions. "Don't stop at the tears; go through to truth" (Goldberg 1986, 10).

Here are some tips to help you journal:

1. **Write fast when you are excited**. Just get your feelings and thoughts down on paper, and don't stop to think or ponder for more than a few seconds. Don't worry about spelling or grammar. Listen for the quiet voice inside you that you may often ignore, and get it down on paper. Don't cross out anything. Honesty is the most important thing in journaling.

2. **Use whatever medium or format you prefer.** A computer, a pad of paper, a smart phone, whatever. If you don't like to write, record your voice. Feel free to make lists or mind maps, as long as you write honestly and quickly.

3. **Any time is OK.** You should start journaling whenever you catch yourself procrastinating because that will help you understand the nature of the problem and overcome it. Some people like to journal first thing every morning, while others prefer to do it as a form of reflection at the end of each night. Others journal whenever the mood strikes them. But try to write some words every day.

4. **All your emotions are OK.** Sometimes journaling can uncover painful memories or tap into feelings of sadness, hurt, or shame. These can be scary to experience, but doing so is one step toward healing. Don't think or get logical. Give yourself permission to experience these memories and emotions.

5. **Write until you are finished.** This may take a few minutes, a few hours, or an entire day or weekend. However long it takes, don't rush it: if you've got a lot to write, it means you've got a lot to say.

Activities

Do as many as you can:

Practice your personal story on at least three friends or strangers this week.

The Moth is a non-profit group based in New York City dedicated to the art and craft of storytelling. Watch some of The Moth speeches on YouTube.

Find out what the level of poverty is in your country, state, and community.

Are some demographic groups in your country hit harder by poverty? Find out what the statistics are and why that is.

Determine what the minimum wage is in your country. Then, calculate what a worker earning that much per hour could make in a year working fulltime. Will it raise that individual above the poverty level? In a single-parent family of three? If so, will it require one person working more than one job to rise above the poverty line?

Talk to a social worker in your community who knows about poverty first hand and ask them what the needs are in your community.

Design a list of interview questions that you would like to ask homeless or poor members of your community about their life and struggles. Consider some elderly people who have experienced poverty. Make sure all the questions are respectful and not intrusive or belittling. Plan a respectful way to approach the people you wish to interview and be sure to identify yourselves and ask them if they would be willing to answer a few questions and be recorded.

Make a creative work about what your country would look like if the five minimum necessities were guaranteed to everyone: a story, a play, a song, a painting, a poem, or a video, etc., and share it.

What organizations are working to alleviate poverty in your community? Visit them and learn what their experience is.

Education is very important in overcoming poverty. According to the World Bank, for every 100 boys out of school, there are 122 girls (Meleis, Birch, and Wachter 2011, 35). Maritza Ascencios of UNICEF, said, "Educating girls is a surefire way to raise economic productivity, lower infant and maternal mortality, improve nutritional status and health, reduce poverty, and wipe out HIV/AIDS and other diseases" (UNGEI). How many school-age children are not attending school in your country? How many are girls? What are some of the obstacles and barriers to girls' education? How can these barriers be overcome?

Write in your journal what you are learning and how it makes you feel.

Further Readings

Deaton, Angus. 2018. "The U.S. Can No Longer Hide From Its Deep Poverty Problem." *The New York Times*, Jan. 24, 2018.

Gor, Claire. 2018. "The Truth About the Feminization of Poverty." *Women's Media Center FBOMB*, August 6, 2018.

Gross, John. 2016. "Purchasing Capacity: A Key Prout Economic Concept." *Rising Sun*, Summer 2016.

World Poverty Clock by country. 2018.

Further Viewings

Batra, Ravi. 2016. "American Economy and its Revival: Part 1." Mar 22, 2016. 17 minutes.

Birdsong, Mia. 2015. "The Story We Tell About Poverty Isn't True." TEDWomen. May 2015. 15 minutes.

Bregman, Rutger. 2014. "Why We Should Give Everyone a Basic Income." TEDx Maastricht. Oct 21, 2014. 16 minutes.

Colenso, Dominic. 2017. "The Power of Telling Your Story." TEDxVitoriaGasteiz. Apr 19, 2017. 11 minutes.

Ojomo, Efosa. 2017. "The Poverty Paradox: Why Most Poverty Programs Fail And How To Fix Them." TEDx Gaborone. Aug 14, 2017. 15 minutes.

Tearfund. 2013. "What is Poverty?" 3 minutes.

References

Barnett, Jessica C. and Edward R. Berchick. 2017. "Health Insurance Coverage in the United States: 2016." U.S. Census Bureau.

Burlatsky, F. 1963. "Concrete Analysis is a Major Requirement of Leninism," *The Current Digest of the Post-Soviet Press*, No. 30, Vol. 15, August 21, 1963, pp. 7-8.

Devashish. 2010. *Anandamurti: The Jamalpur Years*. San Germán, Puerto Rico: InnerWorld Publications, p. 295.

Goldberg, Jeffrey. 2010. "Fidel: 'Cuban Model Doesn't Even Work For Us Anymore,'" *The Atlantic*, September 8, 2010.

Goldberg, Natalie. 1986. *Writing Down the Bones*. Boston: Shambhala Publications.

Kutner, Max. 2018. "The Number of People on Food Stamps is Falling. Here's Why." *Newsweek*, July 29, 2018.

Marx, Karl. 1887. *Capital: Volume 1*, Chapter 1, Section 4, "The Fetishism of the Commodity and its Secret."

Meleis, Afaf Ibrahim, Eugenie L. Birch, and Susan M. Wachter, eds. 2011. *Women's Health and the World's Cities.* Pennsylvania: University of Pennsylvania Press.

Munk, Nina. 2013. *The Idealist: Jeffrey Sachs and the Quest to End Poverty.* Sioux City, IA: Anchor.

Musaddique, Shafi. 2018. "Global Spend on Weapons and Military Increased to $1.7 Trillion in 2017, Arms Watchdog Says." *CNBC,* May 2, 2018.

OXFAM International. 2018. "Why the Majority of the World's Poor Are Women."

Sarkar, P.R. 1969. "Nuclear Revolution" in *Prout in a Nutshell Part 21.* Calcutta: Ananda Marga Publications.

— 1988. "Dialectical Materialism and Democracy," *A Few Problems Solved, Part 2.* Calcutta: Ananda Marga Publications.

— 1992. "The Principles of Prout," *Proutist Economics.* Calcutta: Ananda Marga Publications, p. 4.

Semega, Jessica L., Kayla R. Fontenot, and Melissa A. Kollar. 2017. "Income and Poverty in the United States: 2016." U.S. Census Bureau.

Tong, Yanqi. 1995. "Mass Alienation Under State Socialism and After." *Communist and Post-Communist Studies,* Volume 28, Issue 2, June, pp. 215-237.

U.S. Department of Health and Human Services. 2018. "Poverty Guidelines."

U.S. Department of Housing and Urban Development Exchange. 2017. "AHAR: Part 1 - PIT Estimates of Homelessness in the U.S."

UNICEF. 2017. "Levels & Trends in Child Mortality Report 2014."

United Nations Development Programme. 2014. "Sustaining Human Progress: Reducing Vulnerabilities and Building Resilience." Human Development Report.

United Nations Girls' Education Initiative (UNGEI). "Girls' Education Plays a Large Part in Global Development."

Valentino, Benjamin A. 2005. "Communist Mass Killings: The Soviet Union, China, and Cambodia" in *Final Solutions: Mass Killing and Genocide in the Twentieth Century.* Cornell, NY: Cornell University Press, pp. 91–151.

MODULE 2: A HOLISTIC PERSPECTIVE

Check Your Understanding

At the end of this module, you should be able to explain the following concepts:

What is depression and how many people does it affect?

How can the "fight or flight response" result in chronic stress?

What is the difference between animal dharma and human dharma?

What are the four aspects of human dharma?

What is spirituality?

What is Tantra?

What are three problems with materialism?

What is holistic health?

What are the benefits of daily meditation?

What are seven elements common to authentic spiritual practice?

What is a mantra; in what two ways does it work?

The Social Reality: Depression, Chronic Stress, and Poor Health

In this module, we will discuss depression, chronic stress, and poor health. While this seems to be a very different issue than the economic poverty that we addressed in Module One, we believe that they are linked and have similar causes.

Depression is the persistent feeling of sadness, grief, or emptiness, which is linked to anxiety, apathy, guilt, hopelessness, mood swings, fatigue, excessive crying, irritability, or social isolation. Major depression can cause changes in sleep, appetite, energy level, concentration, and self-esteem; it can lead to thoughts of suicide.

Depression may be caused by many factors. These include childhood abuse, loss of a loved one, financial difficulties, work stress, unemployment, chronic illness, alcohol and drug abuse, rape and sexual assault, among others.

According to the World Health Organization (WHO), more than 322 million people worldwide suffer from depression, and over 260 million suffer from anxiety disorders—many people experience both conditions. At its worst, depression can lead to suicide. Close to 800,000 people commit suicide every year (WHO 2017). While women experience a higher rate of depression than men, men commit suicide at five to six times the rate of women in Eastern Europe (Möller-Leimkühler 2003). Men in the United States commit suicide four times more than women (Statistica).

As with depression, more women face anxiety disorders than do males (4.6 percent compared to 2.6 percent around the world) (WHO 2017). Youth are particularly vulnerable to depression and mental health imbalances, as 75 percent of mental health disorders will occur for the first time before the age of 24 (McGorry 2011).

Stress hormones (corticosteroids) trigger the "fight or flight response." This biological mechanism helps us to survive when we sense physical danger. It also excites us to achieve our best performance. Unfortunately, prolonged situations of high emotional pressure in which we feel we have little or no control, may cause an oversupply of these hormones, leading to chronic stress.

Chronic stress can suppress the immune system and disrupt nearly every system in the body. It is a major contributing factor to the six leading causes of death in the United States: cancer, heart disease, accidents, respiratory disorders, cirrhosis of the liver, and suicide. According to the National Council on Compensation Insurance, up to 90 percent of all visits to primary care physicians in the United States are for stress-related complaints (Salleh 2008).

A British government study showed that *one in four* of all people in that country will be affected by some mental health or neurological disorder at some point in their lives (Bridges 2014). Still, mental illness is often perceived as a personal failure, and the stigma, discrimination and neglect experienced by those suffering from mental health difficulties is often harder to deal with than the disorder itself. As British actor Stephen Fry said, "One in four people, like me, have a mental health problem. Many more people have a problem with that" (Stop the Stigma 2015).

Prout's Vision: Dharma

An important key to our happiness lies in finding purpose, meaning, and love in our lives. For those who are depressed, finding a goal and spiritual meaning, which give focus to their lives, is crucial. If people look to a higher consciousness for insight and wisdom, or, more precisely, what is deep within themselves, they can begin to find the strength and guidance to overcome depression and stress.

When one understands one's life purpose, feeling that no one's life is insignificant, that we all have an inherent purpose in our lives, then she or he will realize that life does indeed have value and worth. This can probably be best expressed with a Sanskrit term, 'dharma.' Dharma is commonly mentioned in texts on Eastern philosophy and religion, but it is often misunderstood to mean simply religion or righteousness.

Dharma refers to the innate nature of any being or thing. For example, the nature of fire is to burn. Similarly, animals have the dharma of eating, sleeping, fear, and procreation.

Human beings are biologically animals, and we share this basic dharma with all other animals. Yet we also have a special dharma that sets us apart from animals. Human beings are not content with finite physical pleasures. Rather we are only truly satisfied when we experience the Infinite.

There are four aspects of human dharma. The first is expansion of mind. We human beings are not content to remain in a mental cage. We want to expand our horizons and explore to find out who we really are. This natural urge is one reason why totalitarian systems that try to limit us and control freedom of thought are doomed to failure. In the context of spirituality and meditation, expansion of mind means thinking, "I am not a small entity; I am one with the universe."

The second aspect of human dharma is called flow, which means merging our minds in the Cosmic Rhythm. Normally, our ego leads us along, but we become frustrated because our individual desires conflict with the greater flow of the universe. However, as a person embraces human dharma, she or he begins to experience the Cosmic Flow, and starts moving with it. Life becomes easier and more joyful, just as it is easier to paddle a boat in the direction of the current than to try to paddle against it. When a person truly flows with the Cosmic Rhythm, she or he feels that the real "doer" of life's actions is not the individual ego, but instead, the Cosmic Consciousness.

The third aspect of human dharma is service to other living beings, where we give without asking anything in return. Kindness, compassion, and service-mindedness are part of our higher nature, which make us truly human. Dharmic persons see others as expressions of the Divine and offer service without seeking financial gain or fame.

Repeated studies show that people get more happiness from spending money on other people than on themselves (Dunn, Aknin, and Norton 2008). The sacrificing nature and service-mindedness of people whom we refer to as saints, show how these qualities deepen as one advances on the path of human dharma. Each of us, as we grow and express our higher nature, serves others because it is our higher destiny to do so.

When we expand our mind, flow with the Cosmic Rhythm, and serve others, we begin to experience the final aspect of human dharma, which is union with the Supreme Consciousness. This is what all humans strive for, knowingly or unknowingly. This is what sets humans apart from other living beings.

It is because of this thirst for limitlessness, for a happiness that never ends, that human beings are usually unsatisfied with their lives. Rich people always want more and worry about losing what they already have. Yogis teach that true fulfillment comes only when we walk on the path of human dharma. By understanding our human dharma and what we need to do to fulfill it, we begin to experience a personal integration of body, mind, and spirit. Through this transformation, we achieve holistic health.

An Ecological and Spiritual Perspective

Prout offers an ecological and spiritual perspective that most economic philosophies lack, but which is present in many traditional societies. Indigenous spirituality throughout the Americas, Africa, Asia, and Australasia invariably revolves around nature. Indigenous people do not believe that the land belongs to them; rather they believe that they belong to the land. They feel intimately connected with their environment, physically and spiritually. Traditional cultures are generally more cooperative, living in harmony with nature and usually treating land as a common resource.

In the last few decades, the environmental sciences have revealed that an inter-connected web of living systems and organisms in dynamic balance exists throughout nature. From the single-cell bacterium to the most complex animal, each creature has its niche and plays its unique role. The environment is the life support system of Planet Earth, a complete system that produces no waste at all—where everything is recycled. As indigenous people know, we are ecologically connected to everyone and everything.

Spiritually, we are also connected, although this is less understood. Dr. Peter L. Benson defines spirituality thus: "the intrinsic human capacity for self-transcendence, in which the self is embedded in something greater than the self, including the sacred" and which motivates "the search for connectedness, meaning, purpose, and contribution" (Benson, Roehlkepartain, and Rude 2003).

Prout values this spiritual perspective, focusing on the personal journey of self-development, and also on service to humanity. This mystical search for truth is quite different from fundamentalist religions that divide people into believers and non-believers, 'us' versus 'them.' Universal spirituality promotes love, while dogmas instill fear.

Besides being a social philosopher and revolutionary thinker, Prabhat Ranjan Sarkar was, first and foremost, a great master of Tantra Yoga. Tantra means "that which liberates one from the bondage of darkness." Including a spiritual outlook and a set of spiritual practices, Tantra is the oldest type of yoga, with roots going back 15,000 years. It is one of the most ancient spiritual paths in the world, and has had a profound influence on Hinduism, Taoism, Zen, and Buddhism as a whole.

Tantra is a spiritual way of life, and should not be confused with the common misperception that it teaches sex practices. It is also not an organized religion. Sarkar vehemently opposed all kinds of dogmas, and went to great lengths to distance himself and his philosophy from Hindu dogma and the caste system in particular.

Tantra recognizes the fundamental oneness of which all mind and matter are composed. It is our awareness of this Universal Consciousness that makes us self-aware. Our own feeling of existence is actually a reflection of the cosmic sense of existence.

Ultimate truths are beyond the grasp of the intellect and can only be experienced through intuition. The divine essence resides deep within every human being. One way to experience this is to use the techniques of meditation that P.R. Sarkar called the "intuitional science." Just as the movements of the ocean currents govern the dance of the waves on the surface, so very deep, powerful but unseen forces greatly shape our lives.

The Problems with Materialism

Materialist outlooks developed historically in ancient India (the Carvaka school), China (a branch of Confucianism), and Greece, later during the European Enlightenment, and finally among modern scientists and Marxists. Western societies are generally concerned with the pursuit of material wealth, possessions and luxury. P.R. Sarkar pointed to the many problems with what he called a "matter-centered" or a "self-centered" approach.

First, the infinite longing for happiness, which all human beings share, cannot be fulfilled through material objects, because they cannot be enjoyed infinitely. When people are encouraged to seek sensory gratification, they spend their energy in trying to accumulate physical possessions. But no matter how rich they become, unless they feel a higher purpose in life, they will feel frustration, alienation and sorrow. Even intellectuals and scholars with a materialistic outlook often run into ego conflicts, as they argue from fragmented viewpoints. This prevents them from developing true wisdom.

Second, self-interest and greed eventually conflict with self-interests of others. Because physical things are limited, suspicion and distrust grow, and one competitively tries to acquire more by depriving others. This exploitation breeds dishonesty and corruption. Much of the so-called "morality" and "justice" of materialistic societies protect the wealth and power of capitalists and politicians.

Third, materialism makes people narrow-minded and short-sighted about the environment. Greed for profit is unsustainable, because our resources are finite, and greed devalues or ignores the value of other species. Both capitalist and communist societies have been terribly destructive of the environment.

Spiritual Activism

Karl Marx wrote that "religion is the opium of the people," meaning that organized religion reduces the suffering of common people and provides them with pleasant illusions which give them strength to carry on despite being exploited by global capitalism.

While this is often true, there is a great history of some spiritual and religious leaders fighting for social justice. In the United States, Rev. Martin Luther King, Jr. led other religious leaders in the non-violent struggle for civil rights—today Dr. Cornel West and Dr. William Barber II continue this radical legacy. Rev. King taught that racial violence hurts not only the victims, but the oppressors, too. Spiritual activism strives to improve the quality of life for everyone.

In South Africa, Archbishop Desmond Tutu fought racial apartheid, and, after that fell, led the Truth and Reconciliation Commission in restorative justice. He says, "If you want peace, you don't talk to your friends—you talk to your enemies!" (Desmond Tutu Foundation 2016).

Throughout the Americas, many indigenous people such as Rigoberta Menchú of Guatemala and the "Protecting Mother Earth Gatherings" of the Indigenous Environmental Network have led the way. In 2008, Ecuador was the first country to recognize the rights of Nature (*Pachamama* or Mother Earth Goddess), in its Constitution. Rather than treating nature as property under the law, this acknowledges that nature in all its life forms has the right to exist; people have the legal authority to enforce these rights on behalf of ecosystems. (Global Alliance for the Rights of Nature 2018). Two years later Bolivia passed The Law of the Rights of Mother Earth (Vidal 2011).

When spiritualists commit themselves to the struggle for a better world, their inner strength and compassion gives tremendous moral force to their actions. There is a popular saying, "Integrity is doing the right thing even if no one is watching."

British mystic Andrew Harvey writes when "the deepest and most grounded spiritual vision is married to a practical and pragmatic drive to transform all existing political, economic and social institutions, a holy force—the power of wisdom and love in action—is born. This force I define as Sacred Activism" (Harvey 2009).

Holistic Health

The word "holism" is the concept that living beings are "greater than and different from the sum of their parts." From the holistic viewpoint, maintaining one's *vital force* (according to homeopathy), *chi* (according to Chinese medicine), or *prana* (according to Ayurveda) in a state of balance is the basis of health. Stress, whether it be physical stress (such as an infectious microbe or an accident), emotional stress (such as anger or grief), or mental stress (prolonged or frequent situations of high pressure in which we feel we have little or no control), breaks the equilibrium of vital force in the body and causes disease.

Powerful Western medicines and intrusive medical procedures can have significant side effects, and, if administered wrongly, can harm or kill the patient. Prout recommends that health care systems and hospitals should offer "integrative medicine," in other words, alternative forms of medical treatment. Often homeopathy, naturopathy, herbal medicine, acupuncture, Ayurveda, and yoga treatments are much less risky and less expensive in restoring health in non-critical situations. The goal of medicine should be the physical and mental welfare of the patient, using whichever treatment works best.

Mind-body medicine is a fast-growing field of medicine that recognizes how integrally related one's body and mind are. Mind-body medicine seeks to make self-awareness, self-care, and group support central to all health care.

First, holistic health takes the whole person into consideration. Western medicine focuses on illness and treating symptoms. Holistic health focuses on the whole person and how he or she interacts with his or her environment. It emphasizes connecting mind, body, and spirit with the goal of achieving maximum well-being.

Second, it focuses on natural healing. Western drugs and surgery should not be the first line of defense. Holistic medicine focuses on lifestyle changes that include diet, exercise, mental attitude, inner peace, relationships with others, and one's environment to achieve a healthy life and enhance the body's own ability to heal itself.

Third, it is patient-empowering. Holistic medicine teaches patients to take responsibility for their own health. Learning how to achieve the health of the body, mind, and spirit allows one to lead a balanced, harmonious life. However, this process takes time, commitment, and patience. Getting body, mind, and spirit to work together is neither simple nor the same for everyone. Everyone's path in life is different. We have many different backgrounds and may hold different values.

Author Dr. Dean Ornish, president and founder of the Preventive Medicine Research Institute, said, "Think about it: Heart disease and diabetes, which account for more deaths in the United States and worldwide than everything else combined, are completely preventable by making comprehensive lifestyle changes. Without drugs or surgery" (Tuso 2014). Modern research backs this up, showing over and over that the foods you put into your body have major impacts on depression and chronic stress symptoms, such as fatigue, headaches, mood swings, and sleep issues.

Activist Tools: Meditation

In the struggle for peace and justice in the world, we should not neglect our own internal peace. Human beings have an inner thirst for peace and happiness. External objects cannot satisfy this inner longing, because the pleasure they offer is only temporary and finite. Instead we must journey within ourselves to find true peace and deepening happiness.

Daily meditation and other holistic lifestyle techniques of Tantra are very practical and can be done by anyone, anywhere. They are keys to personal transformation, powerful tools to overcome one's negative instincts and mental complexes. These tools cultivate compassion, unconditional love, and altruism.

Meditation dates back thousands of years. The process is simple: by closing your eyes, sitting up straight and still, breathing deeply, concentrating the mind according to certain techniques, and practicing every day, one gradually achieves deep peace and fulfillment.

Meditation is a form of deep reflection on who we really are, a process for revealing hidden aspects of our identity. By penetrating beneath the social conditioning of everyday thoughts, meditation frees the mind from repressive dogmas. It can help us see through the veil of legitimacy that exploiters use at all levels to cover their destructive and selfish deeds.

Meditation confers many personal benefits. It calms us. It improves our mental health and self-esteem. It cultivates willpower and self-control. It increases our memory and concentration. It cures insomnia.

Meditation helps us to de-program the lies we have been taught by our society, telling us we are inferior, or superior, that we need to be afraid, or that we should feel guilty even though we have done nothing wrong. It helps us overcome anger and aggression. It significantly reduces the impact of dark feelings, such as depression and loneliness.

With a calm mind, we can truly listen to others. Meditation expands our awareness and increases our tolerance. We can see that others have reasons for doing what they do. It balances and integrates our personalities. It awakens the wisdom, compassion, and unconditional love that frame our true state of being. Unfortunately, this truth runs counter to how capitalist society programs us that we need to compete with one another and win in order to "be successful," and that if we fail, we are useless and undeserving of love. This is a challenge, but it is the most worthwhile one there is. When you begin a meditation practice, you will see benefits immediately, and they will grow the more you practice. Regular practice is the key to lasting and profound change.

Daily meditation clears away the muck that often clogs our minds, making us act in ways we aren't proud of. Meditation makes us know intuitively what is the right thing to do and say in any given moment. When we are not distracted by thoughts, emotions, social conditioning, we can act in ways we will later feel proud of.

Research supports the many health-related benefits of meditation. A comprehensive review and meta-analysis of 20 health-related studies that use mindfulness meditation found that meditators suffered 87 percent less heart disease, 55 percent fewer tumors, 50 percent fewer hospitalizations, 30 percent fewer mental disorders and 30 percent fewer infectious diseases (Grossman, Niemann, Schmidt, and Walach 2004). A more recent meta-analysis of 209 research studies showed that mindfulness-based therapy is an effective treatment for a variety of psychological problems, and is especially effective for reducing anxiety, depression, and stress (Khourya et al. 2013).

The field of transpersonal psychology recognizes seven elements common to authentic spiritual practice (Walsh 1995):

1. Ethics: Practicing universal moral principles is an essential discipline for training the mind. Unethical behavior that inflicts harm arises from destructive instincts such as greed, anger, and jealousy. On the other hand, ethical behavior, which seeks the well-being of others, purifies one's character and fosters healthy traits such as kindness, compassion, and peace. (See Module 5.)

2. Emotional Transformation: This process overcomes emotions such as fear, anger, and hatred by fostering the positive emotions of happiness, love, and compassion. A spiritualist realizes love and compassion unconditionally for all beings. The deepest transformations allow one to develop equanimity, staying positive whatever the obstacles, and experiencing mental peace in both pain and pleasure.

3. Redirecting Motivation: Those who meditate regularly gradually become less concerned with material wealth and status, and more interested in the subtle and internal goals of self-actualization, self-transcendence, and selfless service. By purifying our intention, we gain psychological maturity as we move away from selfishness towards a greater concern for others and magnanimity.

4. Training Attention: Training to concentrate the mind is essential for psychological well-being. The yogis state, "As you think, so you become." If one focuses on an angry person, feelings of anger arise; by focusing on a loved one, love fills the heart. Therefore meditation teaches us how to calm, center, and direct our mind in order to master and transform it. As a recent Harvard University study found, people were happier when they focused on whatever activity they were engaged in, instead of thinking about something else (Tierney 2010).

5. Refining Awareness: Meditation makes us more perceptive, sensitive, and appreciative of the freshness and wonder of every moment. To live in the present, to "be here now," helps us overcome boredom with routine, emotional instability, and cravings that are out of control. Mental clarity is healing and transformative. It develops our inner focus and intuition, allowing us to tune into the subconscious layers of the mind.

6. Wisdom: Cultivating wisdom involves finding meaning and purpose in our lives, giving deep insights about what it means to be human. Wisdom grows as you balance social responsibilities with periods of inner quiet and solitude, especially when in nature. By seeking the company of the wise and learning their teachings, and by ever deeper meditation, we realize universal truths and develop unconditional love for others.

7. Altruism and Service: Selfless service leads to psychological well-being. "It is better to give than to receive," because kindness makes us happy, lightens our heart, and expands our mind. As we desire happiness for others, we tend to feel it ourselves, what the Buddhists call "sympathetic joy." As psychotherapist

Sheldon Kopp said, "You only get to keep what you give away." Meditation shows us the beauty and divinity in all people, and service to humanity becomes a natural expression of love for the Supreme.

These seven elements are integral to any authentic meditation practice. They illustrate well the link between personal spiritual development and social change.

The world needs not only just and democratic social and economic structures, it also needs people who are better, stronger, and less selfish. For this we need to make systematic, liberating changes in ourselves. Revolution begins from within.

An Introduction to Mantra Meditation

by Dada Nabhaniilananda

"Your vision will become clear only when you look into your heart. Who looks outside, dreams. Who looks inside, awakens." – Carl Jung

Please note: This meditation exercise is available as a free audio recording at this link. In early 2019 it will also be available in an editable form in a free mobile app at BlissTimer.com

Why Meditate? Meditation helps you develop self-awareness from the inside out. It is a natural process that reduces stress, raises your default happiness level, fosters compassion, boosts immunity, balances emotions, and can even slow the aging process. And if you're extra well behaved, and very patient and persistent, you might even attain enlightenment. No guarantees.

Meditation was first developed more than 7000 years ago by yogis in India as a path to self knowledge. Recent research has confirmed its many remarkable benefits. The power of meditation to improve focus and concentration are particularly relevant in this age of mass distraction.

Mantra Meditation: Think of the flowing movements of a Tai Chi adept. Meditation is like Tai Chi for your mind. You are re-directing thoughts and feelings to induce a feeling of inner flowing harmony.

One very effective meditation technique is repeating a 'mantra.' In the recording you'll hear a Sanskrit mantra being sung with the music.

Mantra works in two ways.

The sound of the words: sound can have a very powerful effect on our emotions. Think how you feel when you hear natural sounds like a waterfall or bird song. Now compare that with the sound of traffic or construction noise. There's a big difference in the feeling, right?

When you listen to your favorite music, it makes you feel good. That's why it is your favorite. Certain sounds resonate with your nervous system and chakras (yes, they're for real) and induce different feelings. Music with mantra is the quickest legal way to change your state of mind.

So before meditating we often start with some music and mantra chanting. This helps to put you in a peaceful, calm mood and makes meditation much easier.

The meaning of the words: you focus on the mantra in silence and keep repeating it. Focusing like this reinforces the impression thoughts leave on your mind. We want to develop a positive feeling in our minds, so we always meditate on a positive idea, such as limitless love or awareness.

If you become distracted (in other words, if you are human), don't worry. When you notice that your mind has wandered, just bring your attention back to the mantra. If your mind wanders again, when you notice, bring your attention back again. It's kind of like training a dog.

At first you may find that your mind wanders more than you anticipated and perhaps you'll think this means you can't meditate. But don't worry, anyone can meditate. A wandering mind is normal, and you don't have to be an expert meditator to experience the benefits. Remember, no one becomes an Olympic athlete in 15 minutes. (This usually takes at least an hour.) Meditation is a skill. The more you practice, the more peaceful your mind becomes.

For your meditation you can use the universal mantra, *Baba Nam Kevalam*. 'Baba' means 'infinite love', 'nam' means 'feeling', and 'kevalam' means 'only'. So Baba Nam Kevalam means 'only the feeling of infinite love'.

When you are meditating on the mantra, feel that you are connecting to the inner source of all the love you have ever felt. It has no boundary. It is not limited to any particular person or place; it exists in its own right. And it has always been there within you, waiting for you to notice.

"The best and most beautiful things in the world cannot be seen or even touched. They must be felt within the heart," said Helen Keller, who was born deaf and blind.

Meditation Instructions: So let's give this a try. Sit comfortably with a straight back. Make sure your phone is switched off completely. Place your hands in your lap, thumbs together. Close your eyes and breathe naturally.

Begin by noticing any little tensions or sensations in your body. Now become aware of your breath. Breathe in, and as you breathe out, let go of those little tensions. And again, breathe in, noticing your lungs filling with air as your chest expands, and then relax as you breathe out.

Begin mentally repeating the mantra, Baba Nam Kevalam. Feel as though your inner self is the source of this mantra. Your inner self is reminding you of something very important. It is reminding you that deep within you is the source of all the love you have ever felt. It is there right now, and if you pay attention, you can feel it.

If your mind wanders, do not be concerned. Simply bring your attention back to the mantra and continue repeating it. Continue doing this for the duration of your practice.

Remember to focus on the meaning of the mantra, on this feeling of limitless love deep within you. Meditate like this for 10 to 15 minutes.

When you are finished, you can open your eyes and sit quietly for a moment before getting up.

If you use the audio recording, you will hear the mantra music leading into the meditation, and a voice guiding you into the practice. This guided meditation with the music will make your practice much easier.

Find a quiet place to practice and sit twice daily, before you eat. If you make a habit of this you will be amazed at the difference it makes to your everyday state of mind.

"A person does not seek to see themselves in running water, but in still water." – Zhuang Zhou

Activities

Do as many as you can:

Practice meditation twice a day, at least 10 to 15 minutes each time. Making it a part of your daily schedule is the key.

Find some wisdom quotes that inspire you and write them in your journal.

Design a plan to learn what the rate of depression and stress and thoughts of suicide is in your local high school or university.

Design a plan to learn what the rate of depression and stress and thoughts of suicide is in your community.

Determine what the rate of depression and stress and thoughts of suicide is in your country.

Design a plan how to reduce the rate of depression and stress and thoughts of suicide in your local school, your community, and your country.

Research the availability of support groups, therapy, and crisis suicide phone lines in your community and country.

Further Readings

Bjonnes, Ramesh. 2012. "Religion, Dharma, Yoga, Science, Spirituality. What's the difference?" *Elephant Journal*, January 18, 2012.

— 2015. "My Love Affair with Tantra." *Elephant Journal*, May 7, 2015.

Gregoire, Carolyn. "The Psychology of Materialism, and Why It's Making You Unhappy." *The Huffington Post*, Dec 06, 2017.

"Materialism - By Branch / Doctrine." The Basics of Philosophy.

Further Viewings

Brown, Brené. 2013. "Empathy." The RSA. December 10, 2013. 3 minutes.

Gunamuktananda, Dada. 2014. TEDX, "Consciousness: The Final Frontier." 18 minutes.

Ornish, Dr. Dean. "The Transformative Power of Lifestyle Medicine." Symington Foundation Public Forum. December 12, 2017. 51 minutes.

Winch, Guy. 2014. "Why We All Need to Practice Emotional First Aid." TEDxLinnaeusUniversity. November 2014. 17 minutes.

References

Benson, P.L., E.C. Roehlkepartain, and S.P. Rude. 2003. "Spiritual Development in Childhood and Adolescence: Toward a Field of Inquiry." *Applied Developmental Science* 7(3): 205–213.

Bridges, Sally. 2014. "Mental Health Problems." The Health and Social Care Information Centre. HSE 2014: Vol. 1, Chapter 2.

Desmond Tutu Foundation. 2016. "Ten Pieces of Wisdom to Inspire Change Makers in 2016." January 3, 2016.

Dunn, Elizabeth W., Lara B. Aknin, and Michael I. Norton. 2008. "Spending Money on Others Promotes Happiness." *Science,* March 21, 2008: Vol. 319, Issue 5870, pp. 1687-1688. DOI: 10.1126/science.1150952.

Global Alliance for the Rights of Nature. 2018. "Equador Adopts Rights of Nature in Constitution."

Grossman, P., Niemann, L., Schmidt, S., and Walach, H. 2004. "Mindfulness-based Stress Reduction and Health Benefits: A Meta-analysis," *Journal of Psychosomatic Research* 57(1) July: 35–43.

Harvey, Andrew. 2009. *The Hope: A Guide to Sacred Activism.* Carlsbad, CA: Hay House.

Khourya, Bassam, Tania Lecomte, Guillaume Fortin, Marjolaine Masse, Phillip Therien, Vanessa Bouchard, Marie-Andrée Chapleau, Karine Paquin, and Stefan G. Hofmann. 2013. "Mindfulness-based Therapy: A Comprehensive Meta-analysis." *Clinical Psychology Review.* v. 33,6 (July): 763-771.

McGorry, Patrick D., Rosemary Purcell, Sherilyn Goldstone and G. Paul Amminger. 2011. "Age of Onset and Timing of Treatment for Mental and Substance Use Disorders: Implications for Preventive

Intervention Strategies and Models of Care." *Current Opinion in Psychiatry*, 24:301–306.

Möller-Leimkühler, Anne Maria. 2003. "The Gender Gap in Suicide and Premature Death or: Why Are Men So Vulnerable?" *European Archives of Psychiatry and Clinical Neuroscience*. 253 (1) Feb: 1–8. doi:10.1007/s00406-003-0397-6.

Salleh, Mohd. Razali. 2008. "Life Event, Stress and Illness." *The Malaysian Journal of Medical Sciences*, v.15(4) (Oct).

Statistica. "Deaths by Suicide per 100,000 Resident Population in the United States from 1950 to 2015, by Gender."

Stop the Stigma. 2015. "Seven Famous Fighters of Mental Illness." March 22, 2015.

Tierney, John. 2010. "When the Mind Wanders, Happiness Also Strays." *The New York Times,* November 15, 2010.

Tuso, Phillip MD, FACP, FASN. 2014. "Prediabetes and Lifestyle Modification: Time to Prevent a Preventable Disease." *The Permanente Journal*, v.18(3) (Summer): 88-93.

Vidal, John. 2011. "Bolivia Enshrines Natural World's Rights with Equal Status for Mother Earth." *The Guardian,* April 10, 2011.

Walsh, Roger. 1995. "Asian Psychotherapies," in R. J. Corsini and D. Wedding (eds.), *Current Psychotherapies*. 5th ed., Itasca, IL: F. E. Peacock.

World Health Organization. 2017. "Depression and Other Common Mental Disorders: Global Health Estimate." Geneva.

MODULE 3: THE WEALTH CAP

Check Your Understanding

At the end of this module, you should be able to explain the following concepts:

What is capitalism and what is wrong with it?

What is Cosmic Inheritance?

What is Prout's solution to the problem of uncultivated farmland?

Why does Prout recommend restricting the accumulation of physical wealth?

What should be the criteria for membership on economic boards?

What is the best way to organize a public speech?

What helpful tips should you remember for giving a speech?

The Social Reality: Wealth Inequality

Capitalism supports a common belief that many people share—that those who are rich became that way because they were smarter and worked harder than the others around them. This unconscious assumption has never been researched or proven; yet most people, both rich and poor, think it's true. Logically, if you believe that rich people are smarter and work harder, then it should also be true that poor countries stay poor because their people as a whole are not as smart and do not work as hard.

The reality is quite different. For hundreds of years, the rich countries have stolen wealth and exploited people in the rest of the world. Historians tell us that great wealth came from the slave trade. From 1500 to 1875, Europeans and Americans kidnapped between 10 and 12.5 million people and carried them across the Atlantic Ocean (The Trans-Atlantic Slave Trade Database). These Africans were robbed of their humanity; their children were made slaves as well; their culture, language, and religion were destroyed. Slave labor in the plantations and mines of the Americas enriched the elites and helped finance the Industrial Revolution (Williams 2016).

Though legal slavery has ended, and the global capitalist system has changed a lot in modern times, it is still unjust and based on profit, selfishness, and greed. It excludes more people than it benefits.

Capitalism is a system in which people can earn income purely from the owning of wealth or "capital." The more money you have, the more money you earn, often without lifting a finger. Do the math: if someone has two million dollars and earns just two percent interest by depositing that money in a bank, they'll receive 40,000 dollars a year—for doing nothing at all. Of course there are hedge funds and other investments that will yield more than two percent interest per year. You may have noticed, too, that some people have a lot more wealth than two million dollars!

No, rich people are not by nature smarter than everyone else, and many rich people don't work at all.

Another related myth of capitalism is that anyone *can* become rich. You will always hear some amazing stories of a smart person who worked hard, and who became rich. However, for every happy instance like this, there are millions of other smart, hard-working people who will never get that opportunity.

Global capitalism is fatally ill. It suffers from inherent contradictions like growing inequity and concentration of wealth. Committed to growth at all costs, global capitalism has become a cancer, out of control, and lethal to the world in which it lives. It is contributing to climate change and destroying our planet's life support systems. It cannot last.

Prout's Vision: Cosmic Inheritance

Planet Earth, her wealth of resources, and even the entire universe, are the common inheritance of all living beings.

According to P.R. Sarkar:

> This universe is the thought projection of Brahma [the Supreme Consciousness], so the ownership of the universe lies with the Supreme Entity and not with any of Brahma's imagined beings. All living beings can enjoy their rightful share of this property… As members of a joint family, human beings should safeguard this common property in a befitting manner and utilize it properly. They should also make proper arrangements so that everyone can enjoy it with equal rights, ensuring that all have the minimum requirements of life to enable them to live in a healthy body with a sound mind (Sarkar 1958).

Sarkar taught that every living being has both a utility value and a subtler, existential value. Nothing and no one can live independently; every complex human body depends on humble bacteria for its survival. Whether or not we can yet understand the utility and purpose of every animal and plant on this planet, we have a duty to try to preserve their habitats, and not to kill or exploit them needlessly.

Prout's notion of ownership is based on the concept that the Creator and the manifest universe are one, and that the Creator permeates and resonates in every particle of it. Even so-called inanimate objects are vital with latent consciousness. The Creator invites us to use all resources with respect, and not to abuse them.

Because of this spiritual outlook, Prout does not give the same importance to the system of individual ownership of property that capitalism does. Collectively, like brothers and sisters in a human family, we have a duty to utilize and distribute fairly the world's resources for the welfare of all. Prout therefore encourages the protection of biodiversity and natural habitats through reforestation, aggressive control of air, water, and soil pollution, and efforts to reduce carbon emissions and greenhouse gases.

All this represents a very different perspective from the current legal and economic systems of our world. Private property rights and the pursuit of unlimited wealth have become pre-eminent values. In the United States, for example, not more than three percent of the population owns 95 percent of the privately held land (Meyer 1979). In Great Britain, the richest two percent own 74 percent of the land (Cahill 2000).

According to Sarkar, "Uncultivated [farm]land is a liability for the human race." He further states, "In Prout's system of agriculture there is no place for intermediaries. Those who invest their capital by engaging others in productive labor to earn a profit are capitalists. Capitalists, like parasites, thrive on the blood of industrial and agricultural laborers" (Sarkar 1997, 117). Prout's solution includes starting agricultural cooperatives to better utilize land and provide jobs to the unemployed.

The spiritual concept of cosmic inheritance also suggests that the life and well-being of humans must

be society's first priority, always taking precedence over financial concerns. Hence
begins by providing the minimum necessities of life to all people in every region, a
raises their quality of life in a sustainable way.

The First Fundamental Principle of Prout

In 1959 Sarkar wrote the Five Fundamental Principles of Prout in the last chapter of his book, *Idea
and Ideology* (Sarkar 1997). They direct how resources should be distributed. They are fundamental
because all Prout policies are based on these principles, and while policies will change over time, these
principles do not.

1. "No individual should be allowed to accumulate any physical wealth without the clear permission or
approval of the collective body."

In this principle is the recognition that the physical resources of this planet are limited. Hence the
hoarding or misuse of any resource would reduce opportunities for others. Hoarding wealth or using it
for speculation rather than productive investment directly reduces the opportunities of others in society. Hence, reasonable ceilings must be placed on salaries and inherited wealth, as well as on property
and land ownership.

This principle is based on the concept of Cosmic Inheritance, that human beings have the right to
use and share, but not to hoard or abuse, the resources that we have been jointly given.

Earnings should be capped at reasonable maximum levels. When determining compensation, all
factors, such as performance bonuses and personal expense accounts, must be included. The gap between the minimum wage and the maximum salary will have to be gradually decreased, thereby raising
living standards for all.

There is growing acceptance of the concept of controlling and reducing the income gap in the business world as well. Renowned economist John Kenneth Galbraith wrote, "The most forthright and
effective way of enhancing equality within the firm would be to specify the maximum range between
average and maximum compensation" (Galbraith 1973). Some Japanese and European companies already have such policies. Neoconservatives advocate that no limits should be placed on what they call
"economic freedom," but a principle of law is that the freedom of one individual cannot be allowed to
infringe on the freedom of others, and the over-accumulation of wealth does infringe on the economic
rights of others.

Sarkar used the term "the collective body" to refer to society. He indicated that the government
would have to assume responsibility for setting limits to wealth accumulation. It would do this by
forming economic boards. He insisted that board members should be "those who are honest, who
really want to promote human welfare… [by] rendering social service collectively…" (Sarkar 1958). In
addition to setting economic policies and standards, Prout economic boards will also hear applications
from citizens for exceptions to the ceilings. For example, an entrepreneur or an inventor would apply
for funding to start a new business.

This principle applies to physical wealth. Intellectual knowledge and spiritual wisdom are unlimited, and so their accumulation is not a problem, as long as others are not prevented from using
them.

Activist Tools: Public Speaking

Revolutionary speakers do not make a speech; they set the room on fire! They connect, inspire, and speak with passion. This tool builds on your strengths and develops more presence, so that you can connect with your listeners with warmth, energy, authority, and the power to influence.

It's all in the delivery. Learning to give powerful talks is a valuable way to develop self confidence and assertiveness, and to become a strong leader. It helps in organizing your thoughts effectively and presenting ideas clearly and succinctly. Your mind sharpens by researching various topics and your viewpoint expands by learning about people, new ideas, and current events.

Most everyone has some nervousness, stage fright, and speech anxiety before giving a speech. (Some of the following public speaking tips are from Toastmasters International.) In order to minimize this nervousness, it is helpful to follow these guidelines:

1. Know the room. Visit the place or arrive early to become familiar with the place where you will speak.

2. Know the audience. Greet audience members as they arrive and chat with them, if possible.

3. Know your material. Memorize the introduction and conclusion at least. Memorizing your entire speech is even better, if you can.

4. Relax.

5. Visualize yourself giving your speech.

6. Realize that people want you to succeed.

7. Don't apologize—you're doing your best.

8. Focus on your message, not on the medium. Your nervous feelings will dissipate if you focus on conveying your ideas.

The following are the basic mechanics of giving speeches in a nutshell:

1. Topic: Every speech has a point. It is important to let the audience know what you are going to be talking about, and why they should listen.

2. Details: Here is where you provide the facts and details that support your main idea.

3. Climax: This is the punch or dramatic point of the speech; it is what the speech hangs on. It should hit everyone in their heart.

4. Review: Summarize briefly in two or three sentences what your speech was about.

In short: First, tell your audience what you are going to tell them. Then tell them. Then tell them what you told them.

Here are some helpful tips for giving speeches:

Use good eye contact. This is a really important way of creating rapport with your audience. If, for cultural reasons, you don't wish to do this, then look at the foreheads of your listeners.

Use good body posture. Avoid shifting your feet or swaying back and forth, which is distracting. Avoid fooling with your hair, giggling, fumbling with papers, etc.

Keep good composure. Even if you your stomach feels like it has butterflies inside, your audience should not know it.

Sprinkle your speeches with personal experiences to draw the audience into your talk.

For your opening hook, use a quotation, startling statement, question, or an anecdote.

Avoid vocalized pauses, e.g., um, ah, and, so, etc.

Use appropriate hand gestures; however, avoid using them too often in the speech.

Take a moment to center yourself before you begin your talk.

Ask others to critique your speech so that you may improve your performance. These critiques should focus on how the speech was presented, including diction, voice quality, and how engaging the speech was for the person who is critiquing you.

Activities

Do as many as you can:

Find a revolutionary speech that inspires you. Consider the following eight speech excerpts, or others by Rev. Martin Luther King, Jr., Malcolm X, Angela Davis, Bill McKibben, Chief Joseph, Bill Ayers, Naomi Klein, Cornell West, Rev. William Barber, Gloria Steinem, Al Gore, Frederick Douglass, Thomas Paine, Michael Moore, Mumia Abu-Jamal, Vine Deloria, Jr., Dolores Huerta, Patrice Lumumba, Ang Sang Su Kyi, and Che Guevara. Read part of it to the group.

Watch some of the ten most popular TED talks.

Toastmasters International is a club that empowers individuals to become more effective communicators and leaders by regularly giving speeches, gaining feedback, leading teams, and guiding others to achieve their goals in a supportive atmosphere. You can attend any meeting for free as a guest. There are 16,400 clubs in 141 countries.

Research wealth in your community and country. Who are the haves and who are the have nots?

What are children learning about economics in school? Is there anything in your local school curriculum about the wealth gap, income inequality, or a wealth cap?

Study the curriculum of a local college or university. Is there any content about wealth disparity?

Revolutionary Speeches

These are short excerpts from eight powerful speeches. We encourage you to follow the links to read and, if possible, to listen to the recording of the entire speech. Practice one you like; then read it aloud forcefully to the group.

Emmeline Pankhurst: "Freedom or Death"

[Pankhurst (1858 – 1928) was a British political activist and leader of the British suffragette movement that helped women win the right to vote. These excerpts are from her speech in Hartford, Connecticut, USA, on November 13, 1913.]

….Now, I want to say to you who think women cannot succeed, we have brought the government of England to this position, that it has to face this alternative: either women are to be killed or women are to have the vote. I ask American men in this meeting, what would you say if in your state you were faced with that alternative, that you must either kill them or give them their citizenship? Well, there is only one answer to that alternative, there is only one way out—you must give those women the vote.

You won your freedom in America when you had the revolution, by bloodshed, by sacrificing human life. You won the civil war by the sacrifice of human life when you decided to emancipate the Negro. You have left it to women in your land, the men of all civilized countries have left it to women, to work out their own salvation. That is the way in which we women of England are doing. Human life for us is sacred, but we say if any life is to be sacrificed, it shall be ours; we won't do it ourselves, but we will put the enemy in the position where they will have to choose between giving us freedom or giving us death.

So here am I. I come in the intervals of prison appearance. I come after having been four times imprisoned under the "Cat and Mouse Act," probably going back to be rearrested as soon as I set my foot on British soil. I come to ask you to help to win this fight. If we win it, this hardest of all fights, then, to be sure, in the future it is going to be made easier for women all over the world to win their fight when their time comes.

…..

Emma Goldman: "Address to the Jury"

[Goldman (1869 – 1940) was an American anarchist political activist, writer, and extraordinary orator. She and Alexander Berkman were tried and sentenced to two years in jail for conspiring to "induce persons not to register" for the newly instated draft to fight in the First World War. These are excerpts from her speech during their trial in New York City, July 9, 1917.]

Gentlemen of the jury, whatever your verdict will be, as far as we are concerned, nothing will be changed.

I have held ideas all my life. I have publicly held my ideas for twenty-seven years. Nothing on earth would ever make me change my ideas except one thing; and that is, if you will prove to me that our position is wrong, untenable, or lacking in historic fact. But never would I change my ideas because I am found guilty. I may remind you of two great Americans, undoubtedly not unknown to you, gentlemen of the jury; Ralph Waldo Emerson and Henry David Thoreau. When Thoreau was placed in prison for refusing to pay taxes, he was visited by Ralph Waldo Emerson and Emerson said: "David, what are you doing in jail?" and Thoreau replied: "Ralph, what are you doing outside, when honest people are in jail for their ideals?" Gentlemen of the jury, I do not wish to influence you. I do not wish to appeal to your passions. I do not wish to influence you by the fact that I am a woman. I have no such desires and no such designs. I take it that you are sincere enough and honest enough and brave enough to render a verdict according to your convictions, beyond the shadow of a reasonable doubt.....

But whatever your decision, the struggle must go on. We are but the atoms in the incessant human struggle towards the light that shines in the darkness—the ideal of economic, political, and spiritual liberation of humankind!

…..

Prabhat Ranjan Sarkar: "Problems of the Day"

[Sarkar (1922 – 1990) was an Indian philosopher and spiritual master who founded Prout and the socio-spiritual movement, Ananda Marga. This excerpt is from his Renaissance Universal discourse given on January 26, 1958 in Trimohan, Bhagalpur, India.]

We must not forget, even for a single moment, that the entire animate world is a vast joint family. Nature has not assigned any portion of this property to any particular individual. Private ownership has been created by selfish opportunists, as the loopholes in this system provide them with ample scope for self-aggrandizement through exploitation. When the entire wealth of the universe is the common heritage of all living beings, how then can there be any justification for a system in which some roll in luxury, while others die for lack of a handful of grain?

In a joint family every member is provided with adequate food, clothing, education, medical treatment, and amenities, as per their individual needs, according to the financial capacity of the entire family. If, however, any member of the family appropriates more grains, clothes, books or medicines than he or she requires, will that person not be the cause of distress to other members of the family? In such circumstances his or her actions will be certainly antisocial.

Similarly, the capitalists of this modern world are anti-dharma, or antisocial, creatures. To accumulate massive wealth, they reduce others to skin and bones gnawed by hunger and force them to die of starvation; to dazzle people with the glamour of their garments, they compel others to wear rags; and to increase their own vital strength, they suck dry the vital juice of others.

A member of a joint family cannot be called a social being if he or she does not possess the sentiment of oneness with the other members, or if he or she does not want to accept the lofty ideal of joint rights and the principle of rationality. According to true spiritual ideology the system of private ownership cannot be accepted as absolute and final, and hence capitalism cannot be supported, either.

.....

Nelson Mandela: "I am Prepared to Die"

[This is the conclusion of Mandela's three-hour statement that he read from the dock at the 1964 Rivonia Trial.]

...Africans want to be paid a living wage. Africans want to perform work which they are capable of doing, and not work which the Government declares them to be capable of. Africans want to be allowed to live where they obtain work, and not be endorsed out of an area because they were not born there. Africans want to be allowed to own land in places where they work, and not to be obliged to live in rented houses which they can never call their own. Africans want to be part of the general population, and not confined to living in their own ghettoes. African men want to have their wives and children to live with them where they work, and not be forced into an unnatural existence in men's hostels. African women want to be with their men folk and not be left permanently widowed in the Reserves. Africans want to be allowed out after eleven o'clock at night and not to be confined to their rooms like little children. Africans want to be allowed to travel in their own country and to seek work where they want to and not where the Labor Bureau tells them to. Africans want a just share in the whole of South Africa; they want security and a stake in society.

Above all, we want equal political rights, because without them our disabilities will be permanent. I know this sounds revolutionary to the whites in this country, because the majority of voters will be Africans. This makes the white man fear democracy.

But this fear cannot be allowed to stand in the way of the only solution which will guarantee racial harmony and freedom for all. It is not true that the enfranchisement of all will result in racial domination. Political division, based on color, is entirely artificial and, when it disappears, so will the domination of one color group by another. The African National Congress has spent half a century fighting against racialism. When it triumphs, it will not change that policy.

This then is what the ANC is fighting. Their struggle is a truly national one. It is a struggle of the African people, inspired by their own suffering and their own experience. It is a struggle for the right to live.

During my lifetime I have dedicated myself to this struggle of the African people. I have fought against white domination, and I have fought against black domination. I have cherished the ideal of a democratic and free society in which all persons live together in harmony and with equal opportunities. It is an ideal which I hope to live for and to achieve. But if needs be, it is an ideal for which I am prepared to die.

[On June 11, 1964, at the conclusion of the trial, Mandela was found guilty on four charges of sabotage and was sentenced to life imprisonment. He began his sentence in the notorious Robben Island Prison, a maximum security prison on a small island off the coast near Cape Town. A worldwide campaign to free Mandela began in the 1980s and resulted in his release on February 11, 1990, at age 71, after 27 years in prison. In 1993, Mandela shared the Nobel Peace Prize with South Africa's President F.W. de Klerk for their peaceful efforts to bring a non-racial democracy to South Africa. Black South Africans voted for the first time in the 1994 election that brought Mandela the presidency of South Africa.]
.....

Robert F. Kennedy: "On the Death of Martin Luther King, Jr."

[Robert F. Kennedy (1925-1968), younger brother of slain U.S. President John F. Kennedy, spoke before a large crowd in Indianapolis, Indiana. It was April 4, 1968, the day that Rev. Dr. Martin Luther King, Jr. was assassinated. The gathering was actually a planned campaign rally for his bid to get the 1968 Democratic nomination for president. This is his entire speech. After he spoke, Indianapolis was the only large American city that did not experience angry riots that night.]

Ladies and Gentlemen, I'm only going to talk to you just for a minute or so this evening. Because… I have some very sad news for all of you, and I think sad news for all of our fellow citizens, and people who love peace all over the world, and that is that Martin Luther King was shot and was killed tonight in Memphis, Tennessee.

Martin Luther King dedicated his life to love and to justice between fellow human beings. He died in the cause of that effort. In this difficult day, in this difficult time for the United States, it's perhaps well to ask what kind of a nation we are and what direction we want to move in.

For those of you who are black—considering the evidence evidently is that there were white people who were responsible—you can be filled with bitterness, and with hatred, and a desire for revenge.

We can move in that direction as a country, in greater polarization—black people among blacks, and white among whites, filled with hatred toward one another. Or we can make an effort, as Martin Luther King did, to understand and to comprehend, and replace that violence, that stain of bloodshed that has spread across our land, with an effort to understand, compassion, and love.

For those of you who are black and are tempted to be filled with hatred and mistrust of the injustice of such an act, against all white people, I would only say that I can also feel in my own heart the same kind of feeling. I had a member of my family killed, but he was killed by a white man.

But we have to make an effort in the United States. We have to make an effort to understand, to get beyond these rather difficult times.

My favorite poet was Aeschylus. He once wrote: "Even in our sleep, pain which cannot forget falls drop by drop upon the heart, until, in our own despair, against our will, comes wisdom through the awful grace of God."

What we need in the United States is not division; what we need in the United States is not hatred; what we need in the United States is not violence and lawlessness, but it is love and wisdom, and compassion toward one another, and a feeling of justice toward those who still suffer within our country, whether they be white or whether they be black.

So I ask you tonight to return home, to say a prayer for the family of Martin Luther King. Yeah, that's true, but more importantly to say a prayer for our own country, which all of us love—a prayer for understanding and that compassion of which I spoke. We can do well in this country. We will have difficult times. We've had difficult times in the past. And we will have difficult times in the future. It is not the end of violence; it is not the end of lawlessness; and it's not the end of disorder.

But the vast majority of white people and the vast majority of black people in this country want to live together, want to improve the quality of our life, and want justice for all human beings that abide in our land.

Let us dedicate ourselves to what the Greeks wrote so many years ago: to tame the savageness of man and make gentle the life of this world. Let us dedicate ourselves to that, and say a prayer for our country and for our people. Thank you very much.

…..

Rigoberta Menchú Tum: "Nobel Peace Prize Acceptance Lecture, December 10, 1992"

[Rigoberta Menchú (born 1959) is a K'iche' political and human rights activist from Guatemala. She and many others brought lawsuits and testified against Guatemalan general and former dictator Efrain Rios Montt, who was found guilty of genocide and crimes against humanity during the bloodiest phase of the country's 36-year civil war. These are short excerpts of her speech, translated from Spanish.]

…I consider this Prize, not as a reward to me personally, but rather as one of the greatest conquests in the struggle for peace, for human rights and for the rights of the indigenous people, who, for 500 years, have been split, fragmented, as well as the victims of genocides, repression and discrimination.

…The Maya people developed and spread geographically through some 300,000 square kilometers. They occupied parts of the South of Mexico, Belize, Guatemala, as well as Honduras and El Salvador. They developed a very rich civilization in the area of political organization, as well as in social and economic fields. They were great scientists in the fields of mathematics, astronomy, agriculture, architecture, and engineering. They were great artists in the fields of sculpture, painting, weaving and carving.

…Who can predict what other great scientific conquests and developments these people could have achieved, if they had not been conquered by blood and fire, and subjected to an ethnocide that affected nearly 50 million people in the course of 500 years?

…The expressions of great happiness by the Indian Organizations in the entire Continent and the worldwide congratulations received for the award of the Nobel Peace Prize, clearly indicate the great importance of this decision. It is the recognition of the European debt to the American indigenous people. It is an appeal to the conscience of humanity so that those conditions of marginalization that condemned them to colonialism and exploitation may be eradicated. It is a cry for life, peace, justice, equality, and fraternity among human beings.

…..

Emma Watson: UN Speech to Launch HeforShe Initiative

[This is an excerpt from the moving speech by Emma Watson (born 1990), British actor and Goodwill Ambassador for UN Women, at the United Nations on September 20, 2014.]

Today we are launching a campaign called HeForShe. I am reaching out to you because we need your help. We want to end gender inequality, and to do this, we need everyone involved...

I was appointed as Goodwill Ambassador for UN Women six months ago. And, the more I spoke about feminism, the more I realized that fighting for women's rights has too often become synonymous with man-hating. If there is one thing I know for certain, it is that this has to stop.

For the record, feminism, by definition, is the belief that men and women should have equal rights and opportunities. It is the theory of political, economic and social equality of the sexes....

I decided that I was a feminist, and this seemed uncomplicated to me. But my recent research has shown me that feminism has become an unpopular word. Women are choosing not to identify as feminists. Apparently, I'm among the ranks of women whose expressions are seen as too strong, too aggressive, isolating, and anti-men. Unattractive, even.

Why has the word become such an uncomfortable one? I am from Britain, and I think it is right I am paid the same as my male counterparts. I think it is right that I should be able to make decisions about my own body. I think it is right that women be involved on my behalf in the policies and decisions that will affect my life. I think it is right that socially, I am afforded the same respect as men.

But sadly, I can say that there is no one country in the world where all women can expect to see these rights. No country in the world can yet say that they achieved gender equality. These rights, I consider to be human rights, but I am one of the lucky ones.

My life is a sheer privilege because my parents didn't love me less because I was born a daughter. My school did not limit me because I was a girl. My mentors didn't assume that I would go less far because I might give birth to a child one day. These influences were the gender equality ambassadors that made me who I am today....

And if you still hate the word, it is not the word that is important. It's the idea and the ambition behind it, because not all women have received the same rights I have. In fact, statistically, very few have.

In 1995, Hillary Clinton made a famous speech in Beijing about women's rights. Sadly, many of the things that she wanted to change are still true today. But what stood out for me the most was that less than thirty percent of the audience was male. How can we effect change in the world when only half of it is invited or feel welcome to participate in the conversation?

Men, I would like to take this opportunity to extend your formal invitation. Gender equality is your issue, too. Because to date, I've seen my father's role as a parent being valued less by society, despite my need of his presence as a child, as much as my mother's. I've seen young men suffering from mental illness, unable to ask for help, for fear it would make them less of a man. In fact, in the UK, suicide is the biggest killer of men between 20 to 49, eclipsing road accidents, cancer and coronary heart disease. I've seen men made fragile and insecure by a distorted sense of what constitutes male success. Men don't have the benefits of equality, either.

We don't often talk about men being imprisoned by gender stereotypes, but I can see that they are, and that when they are free, things will change for women as a natural consequence...

Both men and women should feel free to be sensitive. Both men and women should feel free to be strong. If we stop defining each other by what we are not, and start defining ourselves by who we are, we can all be freer, and this is what HeForShe is about. It's about freedom.

…..

Winona LaDuke: "Keystone Pipeline on Native Lands?"

[Winona LaDuke (born 1959) is an Anishinaabe environmentalist, economist, and writer, known for her work on tribal land claims and preservation, as well as sustainable development. She was a two-time vice presidential candidate with Ralph Nader for the Green Party. She is the executive director of Honor the Earth. This is an excerpt from her talk at Cooper Union, New York City, on October 25, 2014.]

I don't think any of us had any idea that they were going to retool the infrastructure of this country. We didn't have any idea of the number of pipelines being proposed, the number of bomb trains that would be going by. We are in an era of society which is so addicted to fossil fuels… that we do extreme things to get them.

Extreme behavior is when you blow off the top of 500 mountains in Appalachia. That's extreme behavior. Extreme behavior is when you drill 20,000 feet under the ocean and hope it's going to pan out when you drill for oil. You keep looking for new places to drill….. Extreme behavior is when you frack the bedrock and it explodes ….for short term gain for some energy companies.

Extreme behavior is what addicts do. We have a society that is based on addiction. I've been part of movements with a lot of people in this room to oppose nuclear power plants, oppose Dakota Pipeline projects. What we have done is we've successfully fought off a lot of power plants; we've fought off a lot of dam projects.

There are some pictures there of Big Maps in New Brunswick of a native woman in front of 300 riot cops with an eagle feather. Or pictures of a native man looking at snipers in his village, protesting Esteban Southwest Resources, a Houston-based fracking company trying to explore last year in New Brunswick.

I did not sign up for such a loss of civil rights, human rights. I did not sign up for the military to take over our territories to protect oil. I didn't sign up for drones to protect the pipelines. None of us signed up for that. That is what a crisis in democracy looks like when you have a highly addictive society.

The answers are clear. You don't ship your food around. You don't slather your food with oil. You have an economy that doesn't require so much energy. Public policy on a local level needs to be very diligent all the way up to the national level. We need power that is controlled by us, and not major corporations.

Further Readings

Gates, Bill. "Why Inequality Matters: A Review of Thomas Piketty's book, Capital in the 21st Century." *The Blog of Bill Gates*, October 13, 2014.

Gross, Jagatbandhu John. "Purchasing Capacity: A Key Prout Economic Concept – Part Two." *Rising Sun*, Winter 2017.

Lister, Kat. "The 10 Greatest Speeches of All Time, by 10 Inspirational Women." *Marie Claire*, March 2, 2017.

Sanders, Bernie. 2015. "Income and Wealth Inequality."

Further Viewings

Anderson, Chris. "TED's Secret to Great Public Speaking." April 19, 2016. 8 minutes.
Clifford, Jacob and Adrian Hill. "Income and Wealth Inequality: Crash Course Economics #17." December 6, 2015. 10 minutes.
Oliver, John. "The Wealth Gap: Last Week Tonight with John Oliver (HBO)." July 13, 2014. 14 minutes.
Spencer, Joseph. "Global Wealth Inequality - Did you know this?" February 4, 2017. 6 minutes.
Wilkinson, Richard. "How Economic Inequality Harms Societies." TEDGlobal. July 2011. 16 minutes.

References

Cahill, Kevin. 2000. *Who Owns Britain?* London: Canongate.
Galbraith, John Kenneth. 1973. *Economics and the Public Purpose.* New York: The New American Library.
Meyer, Peter. 1979. "Land Rush: A Survey of America's Land – Who Owns It, Who Controls It, How Much is Left." *Harper's Magazine,* January 1979.
Sarkar, P.R. 1958. *Problems of the Day.* Calcutta: Ananda Marga Publications.
— 1992. "Agrarian Revolution," *Proutist Economics.* Calcutta: Ananda Marga Publications.
Toastmasters International.
The Trans-Atlantic Slave Trade Database.
Wilkinson, Richard and Kate Pickett. 2009. *The Spirit Level: Why More Equal Societies Almost Always Do Better.* Allen Lane.
Williams, Tasha. 2016. "America, the House That Slavery Built: By Minimizing How we Talk About Slavery, We Ignore Its Profound Impact on the Development of the American Economy." *Pacific Standard,* August 5, 2016.

MODULE 4: FOR THE WELFARE OF THE EARTH AND ALL LIVING BEINGS

Check Your Understanding

At the end of this module, you should be able to explain the following concepts:

Why can global capitalism be compared with a cancer?

How does air pollution affect us?

Why is the maximum utilization of the planet's resources important?

Why are effectiveness, efficacy, and efficiency needed for maximum utilization?

Why is rational distribution also important?

According to Prout, what are the three priorities for deciding rational distribution?

Are individual interests or collective interests more important?

What are the physical, metaphysical, and spiritual potentialities of a person and society?

Why and in what way should scientific research and development be redirected?

What is a consciousness-raising group, and what are its three rules?

The Social Reality: Pollution and Climate Change

Global capitalism has become a cancer, out of control and lethal to the world in which it lives. It is unsustainable, because it strives for ever-bigger markets, increasing consumption and production on a finite planet. The drive for profits results in corporations using their influence, money, and power to get around or limit environmental laws and regulations. Each year industries release into the air about 10 million tons of toxic chemicals, of which two million tons are known carcinogens (Worldometers). This air pollution kills prematurely seven million people worldwide—over 50,000 people per year in the United States, half a million people in India, and 1.2 million people in China (WHO 2014). It is contributing to climate change and destroying our planet's life support systems.

Ninety-seven percent of climate scientists agree that carbon pollution from burning fossil fuels like coal, oil, and natural gas is driving climate disruption and warming our planet. In fact, the world has already gotten nearly 1°C (1.8°F) warmer since 1900 (The Climate Reality Project 2018).

Warmer temperatures have caused world sea levels to rise nearly 20 cm since 1901, swallowing entire islands and creeping closer to great coastal cities like Miami, Guangzhou, New York, Kolkata, Melbourne, Venice, Tokyo, Dakar, Guayaquil, and Chittagong. Extreme weather events like hurricanes, torrential rain, floods, heat waves, and drought are becoming more frequent and intense.

Prout's Vision: Maximum Utilization and Rational Distribution

2-5 of the Fundamental Principles of Prout

2. "There should be maximum utilization and rational distribution of all mundane, supramundane, and

spiritual potentialities of the universe" (Sarkar 1992).

A unique aspect of the Prout model is that it recognizes the physical, psychic, and spiritual qualities of human beings as well as those aspects of natural resources.

Maximum utilization is to make the best use of the planet's resources, with maximum economic and mechanical efficiency while protecting the natural environment. Everyone can enjoy a high quality of life if we use our resources wisely. As the American scientist and visionary Buckminster Fuller, said, "We have enough technological know-how at our disposal to give everyone a decent life, and release humanity to do what it is supposed to be doing—that is, using our minds, accomplishing extraordinary things, not just coping with survival" (Fuller and Dil 1983, 212).

Extreme wealth concentration causes decay and poor use of the earth's resources and human-made material resources. Corporate capitalism focuses on quarterly profits, ignoring externalities and using up non-renewable resources. When an elite few own vast land holdings, they often leave them sitting idle, or they grow cash crops for export. Poor rural farmers are thus forced onto marginal land, which they clear and cultivate for bare subsistence with dire effects on the planet.

Supramundane potentialities are properties which cannot be perceived by the sense organs, but which include subtle knowledge and powers, such as ideas, concepts, scientific theories, aesthetic creations, intuition, etc. Spiritual potentialities refer to spiritual philosophy and practices, and the subtle force of the universe, which draws people toward self-realization.

Maximum utilization has three parts: first, effectiveness, or utilizing the resource in a way that it meets people's real needs; second, efficacy, or getting things done in a timely manner; and third, efficiency, or doing things economically, reducing waste, and achieving more with less.

Research and development are key to finding more effective and efficient use of resources, minimizing the harmful effects of production, and finding alternative ways to harness renewable energy sources.

Rational distribution is crucial, because without it, the world will continue to have huge stockpiles of food while people die of starvation. The three priorities of Prout for rational distribution are to guarantee the basic necessities to everyone, to take care of the special needs of some people (those with disabilities, for example), and to provide incentives for those who make greater contributions to society.

3. "There should be maximum utilization of the physical, metaphysical, and spiritual potentialities of the unit and collective bodies of the human society."

This principle concerns the utilization of all human resources, stressing the value of both individual and collective well-being. Healthy individuals create a healthy society, just as a healthy society fosters the development of healthy individuals. According to Prout, there is no inevitable conflict between personal and collective interests. Rather, their true interests are shared.

The results of extreme individualism can be seen in the breakdown of the family and the selfish "me-first" attitude which is sadly all too common in the Western world. A materialistic consumer society pressures people to increase their own pleasures and comforts, while staying indifferent to the needs of others.

This principle, however, does not direct us to bury our individual nature for the good of the collective. Society needs to respect human differences, and to allow people the freedom to think for themselves, to express their creativity, and to form diverse relationships. An important aim of Prout is to encourage individuals to realize their full potential and achieve their dreams and goals. Communism amply demonstrated the danger of excessive collectivism. Most communist governments have been vastly inefficient, and made life joyless, dull, and mechanical for their citizens.

A continual process of education and consciousness-raising is required to help people realize that true happiness comes from overcoming selfishness and doing good for others. We need to balance our individual and collective interests.

Metaphysical or intellectual resources are wasted when people lack education, or are denied opportunities to develop their talents and contribute their ideas because of racial or sexual discrimination or economic exploitation. How exciting it will be when the creativity of human beings is encouraged and channeled towards improving our world, instead of being wasted or misdirected by advertising that tries to convince us to buy what we don't need.

Spiritual human potential allows us to develop peace, harmony, wisdom, wholeness, and lasting happiness. This is rare in materialistic societies. Yet throughout history, mystics of all cultures have dedicated their lives to practicing spiritual techniques to realize this inner treasure and share it with others.

This principle aims at giving everyone and every group the chance to develop their full potential. This requires learning and training opportunities, meaningful work, and a culture that is accepting of everyone and which encourages creativity and initiative. These standards will continually rise as social justice improves.

4. "There should be a proper adjustment among these physical, metaphysical, mundane, supramundane, and spiritual utilizations."

This principle concerns how to make the real-life decisions in choosing how to use each resource. The desire for short-term profits must be balanced with the long-term needs of future generations and the planet. Material needs must be considered along with cultural and spiritual needs.

The traditional economic principle of comparative advantage states that each country should do what it is best at. Sadly, this principle has sometimes been used to argue that Central America is best at producing bananas for North Americans, and that the United States is best at producing everything else! Food First has revealed that every country in the world today has the agricultural potential to feed its entire population (Lappé and Collins 2015). Prout asserts that regional self-sufficiency is the most effective means to increase the living standard of all people. Hence Prout requires that the farmland of every region should first produce food for its people, and only after that requirement is met, should surplus products be exported.

The central issue here is one of holistic development of both the human being and society. For example, in China during the Cultural Revolution and in Cambodia after the Khmer Rouge took over, all doctors, nurses, and other university graduates were forced to the countryside to do farm work on communes. This both greatly harmed the society and underutilized their valuable skills. It is true that all who are engaged in honest work have dignity and deserve society's respect. However, those with developed intellectual skills should not be employed only for manual labor.

Individuals who have developed spiritually, who embody deep wisdom and compassion, are still rarer. They should be allowed to spend the majority of their time sharing their teachings with others.

Prioritizing the rarer and more valuable qualities also pertains to physical resources. A wilderness area with especially inspiring scenic beauty should be preserved as a natural park instead of being mined for iron ore. The burning of fossil fuels is destroying our climate and our environment. To re-establish *pramá*—dynamic balance—every effort should be made to develop and utilize alternative energy sources such as sunlight, wind, tides, wave power, magnetism, and geo-thermal.

5. "The methods of utilization should vary in accordance with the changes in time, space, and person, and the utilization should be of a progressive nature."

This principle acknowledges that change is constant. There are many types of change: natural, seasonal, gradual, sudden, disasters, human-made, technological, etc. Change requires that we adapt, often overcoming resistance, fear, traditions, dogmas, and sometimes the government itself.

The Prout model is not set in stone—rather it is a complete set of dynamic principles to be applied, considering the many special conditions of the location and culture.

Technology has the capacity to both create and destroy. Today, institutions and individuals with great wealth control the direction of scientific research, and use that power for their own interests. Capitalists often use technology to decrease labor costs and to control workers.

The challenge for a Proutist society is to direct research and development for the long-term welfare of humanity and the planet. We welcome new technology when it frees human minds and hands for higher pursuits. Every effort should be made to assess technology's impact and to minimize its negative results.

Activist Tools: Consciousness-Raising Groups

In the United States in 1968, the Women's Liberation Movement began to form consciousness-raising (CR) groups. Similar groups were used in the Chinese Revolution and in the United States Civil Rights Movement. Building on these traditions, Women's Liberation Movement leaders, some of whom themselves organized in the Civil Rights Movement, began holding feminist CR sessions (National Women's Liberation). Small groups of women, usually less than 15, met weekly, sat in a circle, and shared their personal experiences. By relating openly and honestly with one another in these sessions, women became aware that they were not alone.

Participants heard that many other women shared their experiences of discrimination in the workplace, including high paying jobs being closed to them, wage inequality with men in the same job, discrimination in hiring due to employers' concern that women would lose work due to pregnancy or due to being the primary caretaker of children, and to sexual harassment on the job. Many women felt that they were confined to cooking, cleaning, and taking care of children even if they worked outside the home, having to become "Super Moms." Members of these support groups also found they were not alone when they shared stories of rape, sexual abuse, and domestic violence. They began to realize that all these problems were not their own fault, but instead, were the result of institutionalized sexism, that "the personal was political."

Hundreds of thousands of women took part in consciousness-raising groups. Participants gained self-confidence, felt less isolated, and expressed righteous anger at oppressive situations. Then, after ten years, the groups declined, partly because some workplaces had started to open up, resulting in more women taking charge of their lives.

A much smaller variation of men meeting together began in the same decade to explore how traditional gender roles were harmful to women and also to men. The men tried to connect to their feelings as they deconstructed male identity and masculinity and supported feminism.

Lesbian, gay, bisexual, and transgender activists also formed consciousness-raising groups to empower members to "come out of the closet," as they viewed self-disclosure as a means of self-emancipation, as well as a way to raise awareness in the wider society of their need for equal rights. They shifted public opinion so dramatically that by 2018, same-sex marriage is legally recognized (nationwide or in some parts) in 25 developed countries (Perper 2017).

The environmental and climate change movement also uses consciousness-raising to raise awareness.

When Donald Trump was elected president of the United States, there was a huge reaction against his lewd remarks about women. The day after his inauguration, on January 21, 2017, the Women's March was a grassroots worldwide protest that drew half a million people in Washington, DC, with worldwide participation estimated at five million, the majority of them women (Chira 2018). Afterwards, consciousness-raising groups called "huddles" were formed across the United States (Next Step Huddle Guide 2017). Women, and some men, recounted their political awakenings, their fears about being outnumbered in conservative areas, and their ideas about how to move forward.

Nowadays, many people, both women and men, young and old, feel isolated, politically powerless, and unfulfilled. Consciousness-raising groups can be a powerful tool to raise awareness and empower participants.

There are usually three rules: First, the main purpose is to share feelings openly and honestly. Second, no judging, fixing, giving advice, or moralizing is allowed. Third, what is said in the group must be kept confidential to build group trust.

The following list is adapted from the Chicago Women's Liberation Union Herstory Project's "How to Start Your Own Consciousness Raising Group."

1. Decide your focus. The environment? If you are going to talk about gender issues, will you invite only women, only men, or both? Be aware that many people feel safer and more open when they are with only their gender.

2. Find a location. Maybe your home, a library community room, or your office will work.

3. Decide on a weekly time and day to meet.

4. Advertise. You can start a Meetup Group, Facebook group, a website, or create ads in publications. Flyers can be effective, too. Word of mouth is often the best way to advertise.

5. Decide how many you want in your group. Usually 6-12 is ideal so that everyone has a chance to share in every meeting. If you get more than 12, start a waiting list, because not everyone who joins will stick with it. Or form a second group.

6. Convene your group. Introduce yourselves and ask everyone what their needs are. Explain the three rules listed above. Set your goals for the group.

Whatever your consciousness-raising group is focused on, in this age of technology and alienation, getting away from our screens and spending time to listen and share in a supportive group will raise awareness and make new friends. The personal is political.

Activities

Do as many as you can:

Visit an environmental organization and learn about the issues facing your country.

Make a list of choices you can make to help the environment.

Do research about the food that the people of your country consume. How much of it is produced in the country, and how much is imported?

Take a poll of your family and friends. Ask each one whether they feel able to fully express themselves in the work they do. Did they get the education and training they wanted? Do they like their work? Does their job give them the chance to be creative, to realize their full potential, and to achieve their dreams and goals?

Ask around if any consciousness-raising group exists in your community. If it does, ask if you could attend a session.

Start a consciousness-raising group.

Further Readings

Bjonnes, Roar and Caroline Hargreaves. 2017. "Five Fundamental Principles of Prout," edited and excerpted from their book, *Growing a New Economy: Beyond Crisis Capitalism and Environmental Destruction*. Puerto Rico: Innerworld Publications.

The Chicago Women's Liberation Union Herstory Project. 1971. "How to Start Your Own Consciousness Raising Group."

McKibben, Bill. 2017. "Stop Talking Right Now About the Threat of Climate Change. It's Here; It's Happening." *The Guardian*, September 11, 2017.

Sarkar, P.R. 2014. "PROUT Gems: Maximum Utilization and Rational Distribution of Resources." *Speaking Tree*. January 12, 2014.

Further Viewings

"Before Consciousness Raising Groups Women Couldn't Speak Without Being Interrupted by Men." 2017. 3 minutes.

Katz, Jonathon. 2012. "Violence Against Women: It's a Men's Issue." TEDxFiDiWomen. November 2012. 17 minutes.

Klein, Naomi and Jeremy Corbyn. 2017. "How to Get the World We Want." *The Intercept*, July 13, 2017. 18 minutes.

National Geographic. 2017. "Causes and Effects of Climate Change." August 28, 2017. 3 minutes.

Slat, Boyan. 2017. "How We Will Rid the Oceans of Plastic." The Ocean Cleanup. May 14, 2017. 30 minutes.

Uygur, Cenk and John Iadarola. 2017. "The Young Turks Explain How to Solve the Climate Crisis." 2017. 8 minutes.

References

The Chicago Women's Liberation Union Herstory Project. 1971."How to Start Your Own Consciousness Raising Group."

Chira, Susan. "The Women's March Became a Movement. What's Next?" *New York Times*. January 20, 2018.

The Climate Reality Project. 2018. "Climate Crisis 101."

Fuller, R. Buckminster and Anwar S. Dil. 1983. *Humans in Universe*. New York: Mouton, p. 212.

Kravetz, D. 1978. "Consciousness-Raising Groups in the 1970s." *Psychology of Women Quarterly, 3*(2), 168–186.

Lappé, Frances Moore and Joseph Collins. 2015. "World Hunger: 12 Myths." August 12, 2015.

Larson, P. 2014. "Consciousness-Raising Groups." In: Teo T. (eds.) *Encyclopedia of Critical Psychology*. New York: Springer.

National Women's Liberation.

Network of Spiritual Progressives.

"Next Step Huddle Guide." 2017.

Perper, Rosie. 2017. "The 25 Countries Around the World Where Same-Sex Marriage is Legal." *Business Insider*, November 19, 2017.

Scovell, Nell and Sheryl Sandburg. 2013. *Lean In: Women, Work, and the Will to Lead*. New York: Alfred A. Knopf.

World Health Organization. 2014. "Seven Million Premature Deaths Annually Linked to Air Pollution." *Geneva: WHO News Release,* March 24, 2014.

Worldometers.

MODULE 5: ETHICS FOR PERSONAL AND SOCIAL TRANSFORMATION

Check Your Understanding

At the end of this module, you should be able to explain the following concepts:

What are corporations tempted to do to increase profits?

Why are moral principles important?

What are cardinal human values?

Why is just telling the truth and not harming anyone not enough?

What are the ten universal moral principles?

What is the difference between ahim'sá and nonviolence?

How can the truth harm others?

When can honesty and integrity cause problems?

What is wrong with the average North American lifestyle?

Why is service essential for activists who want to change the world?

What are the four key goals of one-on-one interviews?

Define Prout in one minute or less.

The Social Reality: Corruption

Our society values money a lot. We commonly value things by how much money they are worth. A new sports car is worth a lot. A home is worth its resale price. To many people, a forest, unless they own the land it's standing on, isn't worth anything. Tragically, we often value people, too, by how much money they are worth.

In our society, many people logically decide that getting a lot of money is their goal. The trouble is, the more money a person gets, the more she or he wants. Even very, very rich people are often still hungry for more. If you are trying to quickly make as money as you can, you will probably hear about ways that are immoral or illegal. Millions of people are in prison around the world, many of them because of their desire to get rich quick.

Corporations also have the goal to make as much money as possible, or, in economic terms, to maximize profits, the "bottom line." Corporations try to keep costs low, including wages, while producing the maximum profit for their shareholders every three months. The competition is fierce, so the temptation to cheat, to lie, or to bribe, constantly dangles in front of their eyes.

In the 1980s, partly due to the savings and loan scandals, a new type of book appeared for the first time: business ethics. Today there are hundreds of titles about business ethics, and every university economics department offers courses in business ethics. These courses highlight the need for social responsibility and curbing selfishness. Yet corruption and insider trading scandals still occur.

Sometimes our values conflict. For example, in Latin America, the system known as 'compadrazgo,' or godparenting is quite common. A wealthy patron is honored and admired if he or she is able to give material assistance to many people in the community. However, the people who ask the patron for money to help pay for a child's education or for medical care for a relative do not inquire as to the exact nature of the patron's "business." So by giving small donations to a lot of people, a corrupt official or even a drug lord can become a respected leader of the community.

Prout's Vision: Ethics

Cardinal Human Values

Morality is the foundation upon which a better society must be built. However, throughout history, most moral values have reflected the interests of the rich and powerful. Each ruling class has exploited other classes through force and cunning, creating rules and justifications for those rules to suit their interest. The rich have not made rules or moral guidelines to limit their own wealth.

Conventional rules-based morality, expressed in terms of absolutes, 'do's' and 'don'ts,' is inadequate to solve most moral questions in the relative world. If a deranged gunman is shooting innocent people, the Biblical commandment, "Thou shalt not kill," seems out of touch with the need to stop the gunman as fast as possible at any cost, in order to save other lives.

Human history is about exclusion and power. It is natural that people react if morality is imposed on them. When people are coerced to obey dogmatic rules, some respond by rejecting all morality entirely.

This leads to selfishness, greed, and indifference to the suffering of others. A materialistic outlook tends to breed corruption and dishonesty at every level of society, draining economic resources and breaking apart communities.

To find answers to complex moral questions requires deep reflection and strength of character. Sadly, these qualities are now rarer in our hectic world than ever before.

P.R. Sarkar proposed a moral framework based on "practical wisdom." He insisted that in choosing the correct way to act in different situations, the intention behind each deed is of great importance.

Cardinal human values include kindness, honesty, courage, mercy, humility, self-restraint, and compassion. These qualities are considered virtues in every society and religious tradition. Adhering to these values gives meaning and enhances the beauty of life, transforming people and society. Cardinal human values challenge us to protect the weak, avoid harming others, overcome selfishness, and denounce the lies of those who abuse their power.

In 1995 the American Psychiatric Association published a study on criminal psychology. The research report concluded that the most common factor among habitual offenders was the tendency to lie (Galeano 2001). This character defect they share with some of the richest and most powerful people on the planet! Political leaders lie to their citizens; corporate directors cheat on their accounts and tax statements; lawyers lie for (and to) their clients; advertisers falsely exaggerate product benefits; and the world's most sophisticated military forces demonstrate the maxim that: "In war, truth is the first casualty."

Another moral problem facing our society is that TV and film today commonly portray people cheating on their spouse. This topic was taboo in the media forty years ago. By promoting this idea today, the media contributes to deceit, betrayal of trust and broken promises. Family members, especially children, suffer as a result.

Creating a secret life, whether it be with alcohol or drugs, illegal schemes to make money, illicit relationships, or anything else, results in living a lie with others and lying to ourselves that everything is fine. To succeed in meditation, we need a clear conscience. This means being honest with our family, friends, colleagues, and, most of all, ourselves.

Prout recognizes the existential value of every being; this value supersedes the social value or utilitarian value of a being. Hence every life has spiritual potential and should be preserved and encouraged as far as possible.

Throughout history, a gradual trend has emerged to establish a more permanent set of moral values based on the intrinsic value of human life. The struggles against slavery, tyranny, injustice, and poverty reflect this. Finally, all cardinal human values arise from the evolution of consciousness and the spiritual urge to find oneself.

One important contribution Sarkar has made to the ethical debate is his emphasis on balancing individual and collective interests. He proposed ethics and the sense of justice as the basis of idealism and inspiration in spiritual life, and that they are essential to create a better society. Sarkar stressed that while morality is the beginning of both the individual and collective movement, in itself it is not worthy of being the goal of life:

> The morality of a moralist may disappear at any moment. It cannot be said with any certainty that the moralist who has resisted the temptation of a bribe of two rupees [Indian currency] would also be able to resist the temptation of an offer of two hundred thousand rupees… It cannot be said that the ultimate aim of human life is not to commit theft; what is desirable is that the tendency to commit theft should be eliminated (Sarkar 1977).

To restore pramá (dynamic balance) in our communities and in our personal lives, we need a clear code of moral conduct. We need to broaden our sense of right and wrong to include "right living" in the world.

Ten Universal Moral Principles

Sarkar adopted ten ancient ethical principles of yoga (Sarkar 1977). The first five are called *Yama*, which means, "controlled contact with others"—they show us how to live in peace with others. The second five principles are called *Niyama*, which means "controlled conduct for self purification"—guidelines for how to be at peace with oneself. These two sets are complementary, and they are both constructive and positive. Because Sarkar viewed ethics as tools for liberation and not for suppression, he re-interpreted these principles, discarding old dogmatic interpretations. Universal in nature, they can be an effective guide in wisely choosing what to do in any time, in any place, and with any group of people.

The first five principles of Yama, or social values, are:

Ahim'sá: *Not to intentionally harm others with one's actions, words or thoughts.*

Daily life involves struggle and the use of force. The mere acts of breathing and walking result in the unintentional deaths of thousands of microorganisms. Sarkar differs with some fundamentalist religious interpretations of ahim'sá by teaching that this principle does not preclude the use of force for survival, for self-defense, or to defend others.

Prout insists that ahim'sá includes a people's right to resist foreign invasion as well as structural or institutional violence. It does not mean literal nonviolence at all times (as some, including Mahatma Gandhi, have interpreted it) because that is both impossible and impractical (Sarkar 1960).

The most important part of ahim'sá is one's intention. Individually, it means striving to avoid hurtful thoughts, words and actions. In fact, every violent act begins with a thought, so if thoughts of anger or hatred arise, one should intentionally substitute positive thoughts until the angry ones fade away.

Ahim'sá recognizes certain actions as so inimical they must be stopped at any cost. Individuals or organizations that threaten murder with a weapon, kidnap someone, steal, burn another's property, or poison someone are "human enemies." So in the example mentioned above of a deranged gunman killing innocent people, in order to save lives, the killer must be stopped as quickly as possible. Ahim'sá would not rule out killing the gunman in this case if it was the only way to save others.

A nation needs an armed police force and military for its security. Proper training and discipline are important to instill this principle of ahim'sá in protectors of the peace. They must resist the temptation to use their authority or their weapons to punish or kill someone out of anger, hatred, or a lust for power; rather, their intent should be to protect everyone.

Satya: *To use one's words and one's mind for the welfare of others; benevolent truthfulness.*

Prout is based on this spirit of benevolence; encouraging the physical, mental and spiritual development of everyone. This collective outlook is considered the most important of all the ten principles, because it directs one's life for the goal of others. Satya directly opposes the lies of convenience and hypocrisy of those in power.

However, situations do arise when the truth can hurt others. For example, if someone is hunted by a violent mob, benevolent truthfulness would probably favor hiding the victim and lying to the mob when they come hunting for that person. If someone tells you something in confidence, revealing their secret to the world can cause so much shame and guilt that it drives a person to suicide. In other words, instead of simple truth, this principle aspires to a higher calling based on benevolence.

If you always think for the welfare of others, you will develop great inner strength and mental clarity. This will enable you to inspire others to realize their hopes and dreams. In interpersonal relations, the truth should be conveyed with gentle and loving words.

We have a much more positive effect on people when we convey praise than censure. How do we feel about the people in our lives who give us praise and those who put us down? We want to do well to please those we feel are on our side, who praise and support us. We are much more ready to listen to their advice and suggestions, too.

Asteya: *Not to take what rightfully belongs to others, and not to deprive others of what is their due.*

In all societies, human beings have created systems of ownership and laws to avoid conflicts. Prout recognizes the need to question and to redesign unjust laws for the welfare of everyone. Yet when one breaks the law or steals for self-interest, the mind becomes crude—greed, lust, and habitual lying bring about one's downfall.

This principle rejects corruption and cheating, which are especially destructive in economically undeveloped countries. From the very inception of the Ananda Marga and Prout movements in India, their members have maintained strict honesty in their personal lives. Sadly, this has often resulted in persecution. For example, when a member who was an employee of the police, customs, or tax department informed fellow officers that he or she would not accept bribe money, this moral stand was commonly viewed as a threat to the rest of the department. Often actions were then taken against the moralist—he or she was transferred, demoted, or fired.

The mental desire to steal must also be overcome. Otherwise greed, jealousy, and anger can poison us and cause constant frustration and disappointment.

Personal integrity and trustworthiness are essential qualities of an activist. One with ideal character is respected by all good people.

Brahmacarya*: To respect and treat everyone and everything as an expression of the Supreme Consciousness.*

Our welfare is mutually entwined. This is an attitude that is both spiritual and ecological, accepting that every being has profound physical, mental, and spiritual potential. We are each a part of the whole. We are each consciousness. Thus we have the right to object to someone's actions, but we do not have the right to hate that person.

At the end of a yoga class in a prison in Great Britain, the instructor announced a homework assignment: "To everyone you see this week, think, 'I love you.'" One prisoner thought it ridiculous, but decided to try it anyway, as no one would know since it was all in his head. It was hard for him not to laugh when he thought, 'I love you,' as he passed the meanest prisoners and toughest guards. Within hours people were asking him why he was grinning all the time. By the end of the week, both convicts and guards asked him what had happened, because he wasn't getting into arguments or fights anymore. He always seemed cheerful and friendly. He wisely decided to continue the exercise. What worked for him can work for anyone.

Aparigraha*: Not to accumulate wealth or indulge in comforts which are unnecessary for the preservation of life.*

Aparigraha is an ecological principle of simple living with only as many material belongings as is necessary. If you have more than you need, donate the extra to charity. For example, every time you buy a new piece of clothing, donate two pieces of clothing in your closet to charity. Your closet will gradually become less cluttered, and you will probably notice that you start feeling lighter, too. Sometimes called "minimalism," this means to reduce shopping, avoid debt, and give extra possessions away.

Aparigraha is based on the idea of Cosmic Inheritance, that we do not own the wealth of this planet. Instead we have inherited this world from the Cosmos. We are its caretakers, and we only have the right to use and share resources for the welfare of all. Unfortunately, in North America five percent of the world's population is consuming 30 percent of the world's resources and creating 30 percent of the world's waste; if everyone in the world copied this lifestyle, we would need five planets! (Boyd 2011). Ecologists prescribe personal recycling, conserving home energy, reducing automobile use, and changing one's food to a plant-based diet.

Each of these steps requires some amount of personal sacrifice, inconvenience, and time. Education is the best way to awaken awareness about the need to reduce our consumption to help restore ecological balance.

Following Aparigraha is not only good for the planet, it's good for us, too. A wise man from Saudi Arabia in the seventh century, Ali Talib, said, "Detachment is not that you should own nothing, but that nothing should own you." Sadly, many people seem to be prisoners of jobs they hate, of credit card debt they owe, and of lifestyles that are unhealthy for them and unhealthy for the planet.

The five principles of Niyama are about positive self-control, which, when practiced, lead to personal strength:

Shaoca*: To maintain the cleanliness of one's body and the environment, as well as mental purity.*

The cleanliness of our body and our environment is critical to our physical and mental health. Likewise, our social environment—family and society—also has a positive or negative effect on us. Sadly, modern society bombards us with messages about violence and sex that have a very disturbing effect on our minds. Pornography pollutes our thoughts and corrupts our behavior and, therefore, it should be avoided.

This principle also refers to internal cleanliness. For example, eating too much leads to indigestion, mental dullness, obesity, and, in most cases, unhappiness. Self-restraint is important for mental purity and peace of mind.

Santośa: *To maintain a state of mental contentment and peace.*

The dominant modern lifestyle in developed countries is extremely hectic, stressful, and often superficial. Materialism and consumerism stimulate greed, causing even wealthy people to feel frustrated and unhappy. People often shop to escape boredom or loneliness. Investigative journalist Duncan Campbell observed, "Americans have more time-saving devices and less time than any other group of people in the world" (Lozoff 1999, 65).

It is profoundly important to stop and spend time with children, family, and friends. Despite all the problems we encounter each day, we should keep our patience and sense of humor. This is the attitude of an optimist, who always sees the bright side of everything. Yet this does not mean closing one's eyes to the pains and sufferings of others. This principle instills a deep sense of gratitude for all the blessings of life, and instills hope in others.

Mental peace also comes from the deeper understanding that, spiritually, everything has a purpose. This idea is found in Reinhold Niebuhr's famous prayer, that was popularized by Alcoholics Anonymous: "God, grant me the serenity to accept the things I cannot change; courage to change the things I can; and wisdom to know the difference."

Tapah: *To alleviate the suffering of the needy through personal service and sacrifice.*

Giving one's personal time to help those who are less fortunate greatly enriches one's own life. Volunteering in this way is only considered tapah when it is done without the thought of reward or publicity. This type of true service develops mutual respect and instills humility.

Fear and ignorance prevent many people from serving others. By confronting our fears and reaching out to others in need, we overcome artificial barriers that divide people. While serving others, we learn to listen and identify with their problems. Service is essential for activists who want to change the world, because it creates a bond of friendship and empathy with the common people we want to help.

Albert Schweitzer, the Nobel Peace Prize laureate, said, "You must give some time to your fellow men. Even if it's a little thing, do something for others—something for which you get no pay but the privilege of doing it."

Svádhyáya: *To read and endeavor to gain a clear understanding of spiritual books and scriptures, and listen to wise teachings.*

To gain a clear understanding of wisdom, it is imperative that we use our rational, questioning minds. This practice gives the reader contact with great personalities and daily inspiration to begin and continue the personal path to self-realization.

While it is important to respect the spiritual traditions and paths of others, it is also important to oppose irrational and superstitious practices which cause harm. Blind obedience to religious dogmas results in fanaticism. An example of this is the outlook: "Only the followers of my religion are the chosen children of God. Only we will go to heaven when we die, while everyone else will be condemned to eternal hell." This type of intolerant attitude led to the Crusades, the Inquisition, witch hunts, the justification of slavery, and religious wars and persecution throughout history. The principle of svádhyáya asks us to question internally what we read and hear as we search for truth and wisdom.

Iishvara Pran'idhána: *To accept the Cosmic Consciousness as one's shelter and goal.*

This principle offers a reply to the ancient mystical question, "Who am I?" We are more than our physical body, more than our mind; we are pure consciousness, a drop in the infinite ocean of the Cosmic Mind.

This is also an attitude of surrender to a higher purpose. The famous Prayer of Saint Francis, which begins, "O Lord, make me an instrument of Your peace," is an example of this spiritual tenet.

Activist Tools: One-on-Ones

All community organizations are made up of relationships between individuals, and this is also true of activist groups. One of the key ways organizers try to improve the people and associations they invite into their alliances *is through the process of one-on-ones.*

A one-on one interview is both a "public" and "personal" interview with another individual.

The interview is personal in the sense that it often gets into quite intimate stories about someone's life. Of course, it is always up to the person being interviewed as to what they are willing to share. But the fact is that people are rarely asked to share their stories, and many are quite willing to do so.

The interview is public in that your goal is not to create an intimate friendship (although this may also be an eventual result). Instead, your aim is quite pragmatic. You are trying to link this person to a larger group, giving them and the organization more power to make the kinds of changes they would very much like to see in society. You want a public, not a private relationship with this person.

Partly in order to help the people you interview to understand the public, rather than private, nature of these interviews, that you are not approaching them to become their friend, one-on-ones are generally set up in a relatively formal manner. Use a personal connection (name drop). Ask to meet in a place that's comfortable for the person (their office/home or nearby public space) for about half an hour at a particular time so that you can talk with them, get to know them, and help them understand your organization. From the beginning the person knows that you are approaching them in the role of a leader or organizer.

One-on-one interviews have four key goals:

To develop a relationship with an individual that you can draw upon later.

To discover a person's passion, which will help you hook this person into particular issues they may be interested in working on.

To ask this person to do something specific for your organization. Remember: people get involved because *somebody asked them.* So *ask*!

You want to evaluate whether this person is worthy of inviting into your organization. Is this someone who seems reliable? Is this someone who can disagree and engage in meetings without being disruptive? Are they passionate about anything enough to keep them engaged over the long-term? Remember that public relationships are, ideally, driven by self-interest, the need for respect, and a willingness to hold others accountable and to be held accountable oneself. A person may be perfectly useful as a participant to call into a mass action, but not someone you want as a leader.

Be careful about making such decisions too quickly, however. It is really impossible to know for certain how someone will act in an organization unless one has worked with this person. Further, traits like race and gender can bias our perspectives without us even knowing this. Society tends to disparage the leadership activities of people who work more in the background instead of out front like a familiar patriarchal leader. Sometimes the people who look great turn out to be terrible, and the people who look terrible turn out to be great (although often in ways you may not have predicted before).

Prout is so vast that many people have a hard time explaining it in simple terms. This is crucial when talking to new people. Here is one approach:

"Prout stands for the Progressive Utilization Theory, an alternative to both global capitalism and communism. It is based on the economic self-reliance of each region, cooperatives, environmental protection, and universal spiritual values. It was founded by Indian philosopher Prabhat Rainjan Sarkar, who died in 1990. We are part of a global movement to raise consciousness about the need to share the resources of Planet Earth for the welfare of everyone."

This explanation takes about 35 seconds to say. Choose your own words, but you need to memorize your simple message of Prout and practice telling it to many people until it feels natural to you.

Why are Relationships So Important?

Why do you need to get to know someone, and why is it important for you to develop a personal (if public) relationship with them? There are a number of reasons.

First, one of the key mottos of organizing is: "People don't usually come to meetings because they see a flyer. People come to meetings because someone invited them." This is a powerful truth of human motivation. It's much easier to go to a new place with new people if there is someone there that you know. Being invited also makes a person feel more important; it seems like it actually matters if they show up or not. If someone calls you up and invites you and you say "yes," then you are accountable, whether you follow through or not.

Second, people feel a part of organizations and actions not only because they care about an issue, but also because they feel connected to the individuals in that organization. In fact, within an organizing group, leaders will often do one-on-ones among themselves to strengthen their ties and help them understand the inner motivations of the people around the table. The more relationships you have with people in an organization, the more you will feel a part of it, and, therefore, actually responsible for its success or failure.

Third, your relationship with someone allows you to engage with them around their interests or passions.

Fourth, once you do a lot of one-on-ones, the group you are a part of starts seeming less like an abstract collective, and more like what it is, a collection of unique individuals drawn together for a range of diverse reasons and convictions. You start to understand challenges and internal tensions in your organization in more complex terms. Someone once said: *It's not the idea, it's the people.*

No matter how great Prout is, how right you are, you won't get anywhere if you can't get other people together around it.

Finally, doing one-on-ones helps you understand what your members care about. It is by doing one-on-ones that you can figure out what issues will really draw people together in collective action. The organizer's job is to help people develop power as an organization about multiple issues.

Prout includes everything: the environment, ethics, economic justice, sustainable agriculture, culture, education, political action, developing leaders, cooperatives, social justice, the judicial system, and much more. Choosing an issue is a complex balancing act. No issue is perfect. The ecological slogan, "Think globally and act locally," is good to remember, because any positive local action with a universal outlook will contribute to a better world.

Too much study can kill a group as much as too little. Sitting around forever and chatting and getting everyone's unique perspective on everything can lead an organization to fall apart because it never *does* anything.

The one-on-one process provides an opportunity for people to turn their personal pain into public action. This directed conversation helps you find out who they are and how they might fit into your organization.

Anyone who shows up reliably over time and supports the organization is really a leader. A very quiet person who doesn't talk much at meetings may bring lots of people with her, and a very loud person who talks a lot may not bring anyone. And people who will show up early and make sure a meeting is set up correctly can be as crucial to organizations as are those who make speeches.

The One-on-One Interview

Try to make a personal connection. Find out how long they've been in the community, what they're personally concerned about, and what they'd like to see change. You want to use open-ended questions that do not have single answers. Your job is to elicit key stories of the other person's life.

Share your personal story, too (why you care about this community, how you're involved, etc.).

Ask if there are other people you should talk to.

Make sure to tell them you'd like to call them again to continue the conversation (and give them the opportunity to say "yes").

Do not take notes during a one-on-one. Instead, take notes later, after you are done.

An easy way to shift people in an interview, or to get people talking when they seem not to have much to say, is to remember what they have said before. In other words, if they mention their experience in high school, but then move on to talking about their kitchen renovation, you might say, "You mentioned high school earlier. Can you tell me more about your experience there?" If they stop talking, this also can be a useful way to get things started again. You can do this kind of redirection back to things they said earlier quite often and even quite abruptly. Because this redirection is about what they already said, they won't see it as an interruption, or as an indication you don't care about what they are saying. Keeping track of these topics that people have raised allows you to control the interview and at the same time keep the interview in areas that the person wants to talk about.

Afterwards, follow-up with a thank you note or call. Arrange another meeting time if that's what you agreed to do, or find them at a community event.

One-on-One Evaluation: What You Want to Write Down Afterward

1. Give the name of the person you interviewed.

2. Note the different issues and topics you covered in your discussion. Don't post details that seem too personal unless the person has given you permission. State the general topics you addressed. If the person told you any stories, list what the stories were about, in general.

3. List what the person's key passions are. For each passion, explain *why* you think this is their passion. People won't say, "this is my passion," and even if they do, you may discover other passions in the stories they tell. This is something you need to uncover from your own interpretations of what they say.

4. Did you develop a relationship with this person? Why or why not? Would you feel comfortable calling this person back to ask them to participate in something?

5. What seemed effective about your interview?

6. What do you wish had gone better?

7. Finally, did you feel like you developed a relationship with this person? What kind?

Activities

Do as many as you can:

What are the total figures for violent crimes in your country? How are these numbers changing over time?

What are the reported rates of domestic violence and rapes? What are the estimated actual rates of domestic violence and rapes?

Look up how your country ranks and scores on Transparency International's Corruption Perceptions Index. Would you agree with that?

Ask whether bullying is perceived as a problem in the schools of your community. If it is, look up which organizations or campaigns are actively fighting it.

Measure your "Ecological Footprint": How many planets do we need if everybody lived like you?

Take a poll among friends and family to ask, "Who are the most ethical voices in our community and country?" Try to meet those people and listen to what they are saying.

Do one-on-one interviews with people you don't know well.

Further Readings

Das, T.N. "Love in Action: Neo-Ethics for a Cosmic Family." *Prout Globe.*
Lozoff, Bo. "Seven Ways to Fix the Criminal Justice System." *New Renaissance Magazine*, Vol.5 No. 3.
Melé, Domènec. 2014. "Corruption: 10 Possible Causes." University of Navarra Business School. June 11, 2014.
Sarkar, P.R. "Reforming the Criminal Justice System." *New Renaissance Magazine.*
Shambhushivananda, Acarya Avt. "Cardinal Human Values." *Ananda Marga Gurukula.*
"Violent Crime: The US and Abroad." Criminal Justice Degree Hub. 2018

Further Viewings

Leitner, Julia. 2018. "Mastering One on One Conversations." The Arena. June 20, 2018. 3 minutes.
Pope Francis. 2017. "Why the Only Future Worth Building Includes Everyone." TED, April 2017. 17 minutes.
Reisel, Daniel. 2013. "The Neuroscience of Restorative Justice." TED. February 2013. 12 minutes.
Zak, Paul. 2011. "Trust, Morality -- and Oxytocin?" TEDGlobal, July 2011. 15 minutes.

References

Boyd, Robynne. 2011. "One Footprint at a Time." *Scientific American,* July 14, 2011.
Galeano, Eduardo. 2001. *Upside Down: A Primer for the Looking-Glass World.* Montevideo: Picador.
Jarecki, Eugene, dir. 2012. "The House I Live In" documentary film about the War on Drugs in the United States.
Lozoff, Bo. 1999. *Deep and Simple.* Durham, NC: Human Kindness Foundation.
Sarkar, P.R. 1960. "Social Defects in Gandhism."
— 1977. *A Guide to Human Conduct.* Calcutta: Ananda Marga Publications.

MODULE 6: A HEALTHY ECONOMY

Check Your Understanding

At the end of this module, you should be able to explain the following concepts:
Why is going into financial debt a problem?
Which country has the largest debt?
What are the three tiers of a Prout economy?
Why does Prout limit the size of private enterprises?
In Prout, which enterprises will produce essential goods?
What are the benefits of cooperatives?
How will Prout manage large, strategic industries?
How do frames and metaphors shape our perceptions and decisions?
Why do many working class people vote for conservative candidates and conservative causes?
Why is it important to choose winning words?

The Social Reality: Debt

A fatal flaw of global capitalism is debt, encouraging consumers and businesses to buy on credit. Corporations spend hundreds of millions of dollars on advertising campaigns to make debt sound desirable and risk-free. Their clever global ad campaigns and direct mail programs are aimed at every age group, from young teenagers to the elderly. The largest credit card companies have launched campaigns such as "Life Takes Visa," MasterCard's "Priceless," and Citibank's "Live Richly." The goal of these campaigns is to get rid of negative feelings about going into debt. The creative director of MasterCard's campaign, Jonathan B. Cranin, explained, "One of the tricks in the credit card business is that people have an inherent guilt with spending. What you want is to have people feel good about their purchases" (Morgenson 2008).

American consumers have dug themselves into a severe debt trap. In 2018 the total U.S. household debt was more than $13.21 trillion (Federal Reserve 2018). Total credit card debt is now $1.04 trillion. Yet, only 38.1 percent of all American households carry any credit card debt at all. This implies that the average household that carries a credit card debt owes a whopping $16,883 (Dickler 2018).

The effects of debt can be disastrous for families. A 2010 survey in Great Britain found that debt problems have negative impacts on people's close relationships, their health and their ability to carry out their jobs. The majority of respondents with debt problems hid them from their partners, their friends, and their parents, stating they felt "shame" and "embarrassment" (Consumer Credit Counseling Service 2010).

Even worse, financial companies prey on people who urgently need loans to pay for health care or other essentials. Lenders use unfair, deceptive, or shady practices to induce people to take on more and more high-interest debt.

The lucrative lending practices of these merchants of debt have led millions of North Americans—young and old, rich and poor—to the brink of disaster. Because U.S. health care is so expensive, medical debt is the number one reason why Americans file for bankruptcy (Backman 2017).

What is true for people is also true for countries. The largest debtor nation in the world is the United States, with $21 trillion national debt (*Business Insider* 2018). The government constantly issues new bonds, bills, and notes to make ends meet, borrowing an additional $3.8 billion from the public every day. If for any reason the confidence of the world's investors in the US economy were to fail, the largest economy in history would come tumbling down like a house of cards.

Prout's Vision: The Economics of a Three-Tiered Economy

by Mark Friedman, Ph.D.

[A previous version of this article appeared in Rising Sun, newsletter of Women Proutists of North America, Winter, 2017. Mirra Price (ed.)]

Prout advocates a three-tiered economy, composed of a sector of privately-owned small businesses, a sector of cooperatives where most production and commerce takes place, and a sector of large government-owned and operated firms. Let us look into the rationale for each sector.

Small Business

Under a Prout system only small firms are owned by individuals or partnerships. There are several reasons to restrict private ownership to small firms, involving both economic efficiency and economic justice. But some private ownership helps create a lively and varied economy.

It is beneficial for society to give free expression to creative entrepreneurs who can create unique and delightful products and services. These will tend to be luxuries or non-essential items. What are deemed luxuries versus necessities varies with time and place, and today's luxuries may become necessities tomorrow. In a modern Prout economy a rational distribution of income will ensure that common people have enough purchasing capacity not only for the bare minimum to survive, but also some of the enjoyable amenities that make life pleasant. Rational distribution will also prevent the concentration of great wealth with its grotesque excesses of luxury and status that the wealthy use to set themselves apart from others. Meanwhile, the increase in artisan bakeries, restaurants, flower shops, boutiques, convenience stores, and so forth will reflect and enhance a prosperous, healthy economy.

Private ownership is fair in small businesses that depend on the owner to establish character and direction. That point was made well by E. F. Schumacher, the great British economist who pioneered "economics as if people mattered" in the 1970s. In a small business, the involvement of the owner in most aspects of the venture is crucial for success. However, once a firm attains medium-size, the connection between the owner's contribution and the firm's success lessens. The presence of the owner may not be needed if the firm has an effective manager, and excessive salary that the owner extracts becomes exploitative. Under these circumstances, Schumacher writes, "High profits are either fortuitous or they are the achievement not of the owner but of the whole organization. It is therefore unjust and socially disruptive if they are appropriated by the owner. They should be shared by all members of the organization" (Schumacher 1973, 23).

When a firm exceeds small size, its potential impact on its community grows as well. Management may become autocratic, and the employer-employee relationship less personal, leading to an undignified workplace that erodes the quality of life for many. If the firm is poorly managed and shrinks or fails, many people can lose their jobs and the community will feel the impact. Similarly, the owner may capriciously decide to move the firm to another region or country. A larger firm can have a larger impact on the environment as well, and ecological mismanagement can destroy a community. Success can lead to great wealth falling to an individual, allowing that person to wield dangerously great economic as well as political influence. There is a need for greater community accountability and control for all but the smallest businesses than is available in the simplistic "private property" model of business organization.

The Cooperative Sector

Cooperatives of various kinds make up the great bulk of a Proutist economy. Producer co-ops are governed by boards elected by workers at the firm. Consumer co-ops are composed of consumers who band together to acquire goods and services they desire. There is nearly no limit to the kinds of goods and services that can be produced by co-ops. In the Prout system of local economic planning, the production of essential commodities is targeted for co-ops.

The cooperative model provides many benefits for society, foremost being social and economic justice. Human beings resent feeling that they are spending their lives serving the interests of other people, and seek control over their own livelihoods. A producer co-op provides every worker with an effective voice over their work conditions and the direction of the firm. It overcomes the strange irony in economically developed countries today where citizens expect and demand a vote in a democratic government, yet submit to dictatorship in the workplace where they spend much of their waking lives. Anyone with experience working in co-ops knows that having a voice in the affairs of the co-op improves workplace morale. Morale and productivity is further enhanced by knowing that one is working for one's own benefit, and also out of a sense of responsibility toward one's fellow workers.

The Proutist cooperative sector reduces the social fissures and pathologies that result from wide income and wealth inequality. All salaries in a co-op will not be equal, but will reflect the market costs of attracting workers with needed skills. However, the gaps will not be extreme, as workers will only vote for pay differences that are likely to result in higher incomes for all workers. The co-op will also be required to provide an income that meets minimum local requirements. If a privately-owned firm grows to a certain size (a size determined by locally-accountable autonomous boards) it will have a choice of remaining small or converting to a cooperative.

Co-ops are more embedded in communities than corporations simply because their workers, and members in the case of consumer co-ops, are living their lives in the community or nearby, with strong family and social ties. There will be no question of moving a firm to a distant country. Co-ops are more inclined to preserve and enhance the environment, as members will not want to endanger their own natural surroundings and the health of their neighbors with toxic waste. Finally, with a greater stake in their communities, co-ops are more likely to contribute to local charitable drives, schools, festivals, and other social activities.

Co-ops bring purely economic benefits as well. Studies have shown time after time that co-ops can be as productively efficient as capitalist firms, and even more so. Economists who study labor-managed firms find that worker co-ops adopt more progressive technology than comparable capitalist firms.

Workers in co-ops welcome new technology that boosts productivity and safety, and increases the leisure available without reducing income, a near impossibility in a capitalist framework.

We also should not ignore that an economy based in labor-managed firms is inherently more stable. In a downturn, worker co-ops will not lay off worker-owners. Rather, members will choose to reduce work hours and dividends. Recessions will tend to be less severe, and recoveries quicker, as workers are not forced to find new jobs and skills do not atrophy due to long stretches of unemployment. Cooperative associations, along with local planning boards and investment boards, will provide expert coaching and technical assistance to help co-ops remain successful.

Large Government-Owned Enterprises

Economists identify certain kinds of firms that must be very large in order to operate efficiently. These are known as natural monopolies. A classic example is an electrical utility that benefits from having an ever-larger number of users because the additional cost per customer for maintaining its infrastructure declines as it grows.

However a privately-owned power company will display all of the evils of a monopoly—steep prices, lack of innovation, waste, and poor service. Because electricity is an essential service for all, this becomes devastating to the entire local economy. Consumers have less to spend and businesses that rely on electricity for production see their own ability to operate diminish. It is beneficial for society in such cases to allow a natural monopoly to exist, rather than having more than one firm wire a whole city with separate infrastructures.

Most market economies try to address this problem by regulation. A public utilities commission monitors the monopoly's operations and controls the prices the utility may charge. The regulators must allow the power company at least enough profit to persuade its investors to provide the service rather than put their money into another industry.

The Proutist three-tiered economy solves this dilemma by keeping large firms that are essential for the operation of the rest of the economy under the control and ownership of the local government. The government does not need to profit, and can therefore charge prices that simply cover the cost of operation. This is the most socially efficient price, providing for an ample supply of the goods at the minimum possible cost to consumers. Such a scheme is not unusual today, as we notice that most cities operate their own water and sewer systems.

A related problem is that privately-owned utilities tend to avoid serving thinly-populated rural areas where it is not cost-effective and they cannot profit. For example, in the United States privately-owned broadband Internet companies provide little service to rural areas. In response, some small communities have started Internet consumer co-ops or municipally-owned Internet service. It is an indication of a corrupt political process that many states passed laws discouraging or even prohibiting this, supporting commercial providers even though their coverage is inconsistent and high-priced. This is a clear instance of profit for investors being served over the public interest.

The three-tiered economy as envisioned by Prout can provide the economic base for a thriving culture. The requirements of life are met for all, banishing severe economic insecurity to a dark past. The creative and diverse private small business sector brings delight to communities. The cooperative sector, where most economic activity takes place, provides innovative goods and services along with the necessities at competitive prices. It also provides secure employment that is meaningful and fulfilling as workers take emotional as well as economic ownership of their firms. Society is also served well by having its businesses deeply invested in the well-being of communities. The local government-owned sector of large firms will support the rest of the economy with essential services.

Activist Tools: Winning Words

We would like to think that we're in control of all of our perceptions and our decisions. The suggestion that we may have been manipulated into buying something, whether it's clothing or political rhetoric, is repugnant.

Yet it happens all the time. Why? Because as human beings, we have strong emotions that shape our perceptions and influence our opinions. Cognitive linguist George Lakoff asserts that most thought lies below the level of consciousness. He argues that our political decisions are not rational, but are filtered through unconscious metaphors that shape our thinking about everything from how children should be raised to how nature should be regarded to how the government should be run (Lakoff 2016).

Frames and Metaphors

Framing and the use of metaphor is necessary to say what we believe. A metaphor is a figure of speech in which one idea stands for another idea. A famous metaphor is:

> All the world's a stage,
> And all the men and women merely players;
> They have their exits and their entrances... (William Shakespeare, *As You Like It*, 2/7).

In *Metaphors We Live By*, George Lakoff and Mark Johnson (2011) assert that many conceptual metaphors are largely unconscious. A conceptual metaphor, which is so prevalent that it is often unconscious, is 'time is money.' Many of us budget our time, try not to waste time, and want to save time. Every time we think of losing time, getting bogged down on a project, or being at a crossroads in a relationship, we are unconsciously activating a conceptual metaphor circuit (frame) in our brain. We then often make decisions and live according to these metaphors (Lakoff 2018).

A frame is how something is presented. It influences the way we think about ideas. We can think of this as seeing the world through tinted glasses. For example, the following two statements can have different effects on people.

> Those who contract a certain disease have a ten percent chance of dying.
> Those who contract a certain disease have a ninety percent chance of survival.

Though the information is the same, people who read the first frame often feel more worried about this disease than do those who read just the second frame. The difference is only in the way the idea is framed (Tannen, 1993).

It is a false notion that reason is conscious, universal, logical, literal, and unemotional. We think that if we merely provide the facts and figures on any issue, that people will grasp our meaning and will reason to the right conclusion. According to Lakoff, this is not accurate for the following reasons:

1. Ninety-eight percent of thought lies below the conscious level.

2. Reason requires emotion. Studies have shown that people who had brain injuries which disabled the parts of their brains which control emotions were unable to reason.ś

3. We have different world views. Politics is about morality, not issues. Politicians propose policies they feel are right. People can be bi-conceptual, and can hold views, some of which are progressive and some of which are conservative. Progressives can be progressive in one area, but conservative in another area. There is no line dividing the Left from the Right, nor is there a political ideology of the Middle.

4. We always think in frames. Framing and the use of metaphor is necessary so we can say what we believe. Every word is defined with respect to a frame. If we say a word, it activates a frame. For example, when President Richard Nixon said, "I am not a crook," most everyone who heard that immediately thought of him as a crook. This is because 'crook' activates the frame of 'crook' in our brains, and so people associated Nixon with 'crook'. When President Donald Trump constantly called his opponent Hillary Clinton a crook, she became associated with that frame in the minds of the public, especially, to people who did not have positive frames in place about Clinton (Lakoff, Smiley Interview 2017). As in formal debates, and according to linguist Deborah Tannen in *The Argument Culture*, there are always two sides on each issue, a pro and a con (Tannen 1998). To have two positions, you must use the same frame for both issues. Therefore, a frame will be set from the perspective of one of the two positions. The corporate-owned media in the United States frames debates on all major issues between the conservative Republican Party and more liberal Democratic Party (Cohen 2004).

For example, for the Iraq War, the Republicans stated:

The United States has vital interests in Iraq (oil).
The War on Terror was authorized by Congress based on the best available information.
The War on Terror is winnable.

The Democrats said:

The war does not serve the national interests.
The war is based on false information; Iraq had no weapons of mass destruction.
The war is unwinnable.

The media frames the debate, using the same terms so that people can understand the two positions. The Republican frame sounds coherent and consistent. By negating that frame, the Democrats activate it, empowering the Republican terms, 'national interests' 'information', and 'winnable' (even if it is 'unwinnable'). Calling the War on Terror an 'invasion' and an 'occupation' gives a much different image, because an invasion sounds criminal and an occupation does not sound 'winnable.' This terminology (our public 'interests' and 'best information available' although from unreliable intelligence) wedded 9-11 terrorism with the Saddam Hussein regime in Iraq in the minds of the American public. The United States began waging war on Iraq in 2003, finally toppling the government in 2011 (Lakoff 2004).

Frames are in your brain. Once frames are there, you cannot erase them. All you can do is create alternative framing or add to the frame, like expanding it by triggering the empathy neural network in your brain.

The Political Climate

In the United States, many working class people are conservative and vote for conservative candidates and conservative causes. Rabbi Michael Lerner led a research team with grants from the National Institute of Mental Health to study this (Lerner 2002). He found this happens for several reasons. First, because people need meaning and purpose in their lives. They vote based on their moral values. Conservative churches talk about the breakdown and crisis in families and in the country, and say that the cause is selfishness. The Left rarely, if ever, mentions this issue. Conservative churches also offer their members a feeling of belonging and connection.

Capitalism gives people a lot of pain, frustration, and stress in the family, because it makes the majority who are not succeeding feel that it is their own fault. Many people feel it's their fault if they cannot find a job. Why? Meaningful work is a human right. It is society's duty to provide an honest, meaningful job with an adequate wage for every person who wants it.

The second way that the Right wins support is that it argues that selfishness in our society arises from "special interest groups"—immigrants, women, LGBTQ, Blacks, Muslims, etc. They claim that if these groups get more rights and more access, working class white people will lose the little that they have. This allows frustrated working class people to shift their sense of self-blame for their lack of success and "not being enough" onto a social problem caused by other groups. It allows people to understand the pain they feel without having to blame themselves.

During the 2016 presidential campaign, Hillary Clinton said, "you could put half of Trump's supporters into what I call the 'basket of deplorables.' Right? They're racist, sexist, homophobic, xenophobic, Islamophobic—you name it" (Holan 2016). In this way, she insulted her political opponents. Today many opponents of President Trump say that those who voted for him are stupid or worse. Some on the Left also dismiss all people who are religious as ignorant or just plain stupid. If you insult someone, you will never win that person over to your side.

The political climate in the United States and in other countries is becoming very loud and polarized, which is shaking many people out of their passive comfort zones.

How Conservatives Manipulate Public Opinion

Conservatives in the United States have spent decades defining their ideas, carefully selecting the language with which to present them, and building the Fox News Network as an infrastructure to communicate them. Conservative advisor Frank Luntz is a master of opinion polls and using focus groups to find out what words resonate with people and sway them. He has advised Republicans to alter their political language in the following ways:
- Instead of talking about 'smaller government', they should talk about 'more efficient and effective government', which appeals to more people today. Government spending should be condemned by calling it 'waste.'
- Instead of 'tax reform', talk about making the IRS tax code simpler, flatter, and fairer. People hate the complexity of the U.S. tax code. Inheritance tax should be condemned as 'death tax.'
- Instead of mentioning drilling for oil or fracking for gas, Luntz proposes using the phrase 'energy exploration.'
- Whereas healthcare is something everyone wants, guaranteeing it to everyone should be condemned by conservatives as 'government takeover.'

- Rather than discussing economic opportunity and growth, Republicans should talk about creating a healthier and more secure economy. Logically, everyone should benefit if 'economic health' is restored. And while economic opportunity would be nice, security is a necessity.
- Instead of talking about curbing crime, discuss public safety, appealing to people's primal needs to be safe and secure.
- Today many people in the United States have a negative image from the word "capitalism." Luntz suggests that conservatives should avoid the word, and instead call capitalists 'job creators' and bonuses for super-rich corporate executives as 'pay for performance.' Most interesting of all, he advises conservatives to call capitalism itself 'economic freedom.' 'Freedom' which sounds very positive to almost everyone, here means 'freedom to accumulate wealth without limits or taxes' (Luntz 2007, Abadi 2017).

Choose Winning Words

As activists, we want to appeal not just to fellow activists or to a small segment of society; we want to reach everyone with our message. Our words should appeal to both those on the political Left and the political Right.

Because we all have implicit biases and differing worldviews, we understand things differently. In order to change people's minds, it is necessary to use language to activate your worldview in someone else by activating the frame which filters their understanding. If we trigger an empathy neural network in someone by continually engaging them at times when they feel connection with others, we can assist in helping change frames in their brains (Lakoff, Smiley Interview 2017).

An inspiring example of someone changing their outlook and overcoming prejudice is in the story of Ku Klux Klan leader C.P. Ellis, who, in 1971 in Durham, North Carolina, co-chaired an initiative to desegregate Durham schools, with civil rights activist Ann Atwater. As a result of this odd partnership, Ellis became a lifelong friend of Atwater's, even though her African-American community and his white supremacist friends were both appalled at their alliance. Atwater has said that she knew Ellis was changing his hatred for Blacks when she saw him tapping his foot to gospel music sung at the end of one of their meetings. In this case, the words of a song helped change a racist leader's frame. As a result of his work with Atwater, Ellis renounced the Ku Klux Klan, became a labor organizer and an admirer of Martin Luther King, Jr. (Leonard, 2016).

We cannot persuade someone with mere logic, if they have a contrary world view. We persuade by reinforcing their humanity and activating the benevolent parts of their brain.

The bottom line is to frame language in a way that resonates with people and activates internal, subconscious frames. Most of the frames that people hold are embedded in their subconscious.

Here are some words that trigger positive frames in almost everyone: decency, fair play, safety, security, trust, respect, freedom, family values, honesty, truth, win-win, love, happiness, belonging, level playing field, practical, peace of mind, integrity, honor, responsibility, justice, harmony, transparency, hope, prosperity, and change.

Using some of George Lakoff's ideas as a model, we need to (1) build an effective communication system, (2) communicate our general progressive value system, (3) repeat the truths that reveal what is right about those values, and (4) act to promote the sense of courage, confidence, and hope that allows the truth to be meaningful and powerful.

For example, to stop oil drilling in the Arctic, name a single truth: oil companies destroy the planet for their short term profit. Point out that when there are oil spills and pipeline leaks, livelihoods of people in the affected areas are compromised. People's personal safety is put at jeopardy. Many animals are injured and killed. The government wastes money cleaning up the environmental disaster. These points activate people's mental frames for safety, security, and financial well-being. This takes the debate to a personal level rather than framing it as an issue for a clean environment, which is much more abstract.

Conclusion

Truths are made meaningful by values, which are wedded to them. Make truths matter. Win with words that resonate by activating already existing frames, by using words that embody moral values, and by respecting each person in your audiences.

Slogans

Brief, moving slogans, about 5-12 words each, can inspire people and awaken their curiosity. If your group is attending a large march, a banner three or four meters long of cloth or canvas can be stretched in front of your group. Additional people can hold high a stick with two signs back-to-back with different slogans, so by turning the stick, people in every direction can see your messages. The more signs and slogans, the better. Every banner and sign should say in small letters at the bottom the name of your organization with the web page, so that those who are nearby can read it.

Invite those who will march to come the night before for a sign-making party. Give them the following list of slogans, and invite them to choose the ones they like best or make up their own. Some slogans translate well into other languages. If the signs are large and well made, they will get media coverage and will be seen and read by both the protesters and the public. The same banners and signs can be saved and used again in other demonstrations and rallies in the future.

Whereas many signs and banners of other groups protest against what is wrong (such as war, corruption, and exploitation), Prout's messages are mostly positive and inspiring, offering hope to the people.

A new vision for all living beings.
Action makes a person great.
Basic necessities for all.
Be a flame in the darkness.
Be a revolutionary guided by great feelings of love. - Che
"Be the change you want to see in the world." - Gandhi
The best happily ever after—equality for all!
Birds need two wings to fly—society needs women's equal and full participation.
Capitalism: Good for the rich, disaster for the poor.
Capitalist greed is a mental disease—try Prout.
Capitalist greed is destroying our planet!
Co-ops are self-help, not charity.
Co-ops create jobs: 100+ million, more than corporations.
Co-ops empower people to decide their own future.
Cooperatives build a better world.
Co-ops are enterprises with a soul.
Co-ops are the businesses of the future.
Corporate stores give your money to rich investors—buy local!

Cultural freedom, economic freedom, spiritual freedom!

Each person here = thousands suffering from global capitalism.

Economic democracy through co-ops, regional self-sufficiency.

Economic democracy: Co-ops of the people, by the people, and for the people!

Economic democracy empowers people and communities.

Economic democracy: Economy of the people, by the people, and for the people!

Economic liberation for all.

Economics from the heart

Education and jobs will free all women from economic dependence.

End hunger—there's enough food on earth, but not enough will.

Ending repressive regimes starts at home.

Exploitation no more!

Fight for justice, meditate for inner peace.

For personal and planetary transformation

For the good of all beings

Globalize humanity—localize the economy.

Globalize solidarity.

Grow your local economy.

Human beings of the world—unite!

Humanity is one and indivisible.

Meaningful jobs with "living wages" is our right.

Money is a human invention; we CAN change the rules.

Neohumanism: Love for humanity and all living beings

One billion people aren't wrong: Co-ops work!

One people, one planet, one future

Our culture is our strength!

Planet Earth has enough for everyone if we share.

Prout: Alternative to "global colonialism"!

Rational distribution of wealth, basic necessities for all

Real education leads to liberation.

Real solutions for a better world.

Real wealth comes from within.

Revolution = total transformation.

Save an endangered species: Humans!

Self-reliance, cooperatives, and spirituality

Share the wealth through local economies.

Sharing the wealth of our planet

Support credit unions, not big banks.

The force that guides the stars guides you, too.

There's enough for everyone's needs, not for everyone's greed!

"There's no chance for the welfare of the world unless the condition of women improves." - P.R. Sarkar

Think globally, act locally.

Together we can build a better world.

Transform yourself and transform the world.
Uniting communities for local self-reliance
Unity in diversity!
We are all connected.
We are all together in this world.
We are one universal family.
We belong to the universe—consciousness is within you.
We have a dream—food for all, jobs for all!
We need a cap on wealth.
Where every life matters
Working together for a new world

Activities

Do as many as you can:

Find out how much personal debt the people of your country have.

Find out whether outsiders control the economy in your community. If so, to what extent? How many of the popular stores, restaurants, banks, and entertainment centers are locally owned and how many are part of a national or international chain?

Talk with a small business owner. Ask how many small businesses there are in your community and how they are doing. What problems are they facing?

Find out whether there are public utilities in your community. If so, how are they doing?

Find out whether houses and apartment rents in your community are affordable or expensive.

Find examples of how political leaders in your country use words and phrases (sound bites) to emotionally convince the people to support them.

What are some of your favorite slogans? Brainstorm ways that you could get your slogans to the public.

Further Readings

Business Management Ideas. "State Enterprises: Meaning, Characteristics and Objectives."

Insler, Shannon. 2017. "The Mental Toll of Student Debt: What Our Survey Shows." September 7, 2017.

Novotney, Amy. 2013. "Facing Up to Debt." American Psychological Association, *gradPSYCH Magazine*, January 2013, 32.

Further Viewings

Frieze, Deborah. 2015. "How I Became a Localist." TEDxJamaicaPlain. December 17, 2015. 12 minutes.

Jubilee Debt Campaign. 2009. "Toxic Debt." July 3, 2009. 2 minutes.

Prairie Public Broadcasting. 2011. "The State Bank of North Dakota." January 24, 2011. 26 minutes.

Reich, Robert. 2018. "In Conversation with George Lakoff: Language and Politics." Inequality Media. February 14, 2018. 26 minutes.

Yunus, Muhammad. 2012. "A History of Microfinance." TedxVienna. January 18, 2012. 23 minutes.

References

Abadi, Mark. 2017. "Democrats and Republicans Speak Different Languages—and It Helps Explain Why We're So Divided." Business Insider, August 11, 2017.

Backman, Maurie. 2017. "This is the No. 1 Reason Americans File for Bankruptcy." *USA Today,* May 5, 2017.

Business Insider. 2018. "The US Debt Surpasses $21 Trillion—But That Won't Bother Credit Agencies." *The Fiscal Times,* April 28, 2018.

Butler, Katy. 2004. "Winning Words." *Sierra Club Magazine*, July-August, 2004.

Cohen, Adam. 2004. "Why the Democrats Need to Stop Thinking About Elephants." *New York Times,* November 15, 2004.

Consumer Credit Counseling Service. 2010. "Survey Reveals High Human Cost of Debt Problems." July 21, 2010.

Dickler, Jessica. 2018. "Credit Card Debt Hits a Record High. It's Time to Make a Payoff Plan." *CNBC,* January 23, 2018.

Federal Reserve Bank of New York. 2018. "Household Debt and Credit Report." Center for Microeconomic Data. Q1.

Holan, Angie. 2016. "In Context: Hillary Clinton and the 'Basket of Deplorables'" Politifact Online. September 11, 2016.

Lakoff, George. 2004. *Don't Think of an Elephant! Know Your Values and Frame the Debate: The Essential Guide for Progressives.* Chelsea Green Publishing.

— 2016. "Defending Freedom: A Response to Steven Pinker." *New Republic online,* February 24, 2016.

— 2018. "What Scientific Concept Would Improve Everybody's Toolkit?" Edge.org. September 17, 2018.

— and Mark Johnson. 2011. *Metaphors We Live By.* Chicago: U. of Chicago Press.

Leonard, Teresa. 2016. "Civil Rights Activist and Klan Leader Attacked Problem from Opposite Sides." newsobserver.com. June 24, 2016. Lerner, Michael. 2002. *Spirit Matters.* Newburyport, MA: Hampton Roads.

Luntz, Frank. 2007. *Words That Work*: *It's Not What You Say, It's What People Hear.* Revised, Updated Edition. Hyperion e-Books: January 2, 2007.

MacFarquhar, Larissa. 1998. "Thank you for Not Fighting: Deborah Tannen Wants Us to be Nice." *New York Times*, April 5, 1998.

Morgenson, Gretchen. 2008. "Given a Shovel, Americans Dig Deeper Into Debt." *The New York Times,* July 20, 2008.

Rosenberg, Paul. 2017. "Linguist George Lakoff Explains how the Democrats Helped Elect Trump." *Salon.* Alternet. January 16, 2017.

Schumacher, E.F. 1973. *Small is Beautiful: A Study of Economics As If People Mattered.* London: Abacus.

Tannen, Deborah. ed. 1993. *Framing in Discourse.* Oxford: Oxford University Press.

— 1998. *The Argument Culture: Stopping America's War of Words.* New York: Ballantine Books.

MODULE 7: COOPERATIVES CAN CREATE JOBS FOR ALL

Check Your Understanding

At the end of this module, you should be able to explain the following concepts:

How do economists define unemployment and underemployment?

What is a cooperative?

How many people in the world are members of co-ops? How many work for co-ops?

What are the three requirements for co-ops to be successful?

What are the benefits of a cooperative market economy?

Why do co-ops hold a competitive advantage over both private and public enterprises?

How do worker co-ops function?

What are credit unions; how many are there in the world?

How do co-ops benefit the community where they are?

How do you start a successful co-op?

The Social Reality: Unemployment

Economists everywhere have an odd way of defining unemployment. In the United States, the unemployed are defined as people who are without jobs and who have actively looked for work within the past four weeks. Economists do not count the chronically unemployed who have given up hope and stopped looking. They also don't count those who are child-rearing, are taking care of relatives, are ill, or are in school. They do not take into account people who are underemployed, for example, those who only have part-time or temporary work. Finally, they do not note whether the wages paid for work are enough to survive—many low-paid employees need two or even three jobs to support their families.

In the United States, unemployment among African-American youth is at 50 percent, much higher than in the general public (Elejalde-Ruiz 2018).

Among the 19,000 Lakota people on the Pine Ridge Indian Reservation, unemployment was 89 percent (Re-Member 2018). Many communities, regions, and even countries are suffering economic depression.

Anyone in the world who wants to work but cannot find a full time job that pays a living wage is facing economic depression. The loss of a job is not merely the loss of a paycheck, but it is also the loss of a routine, security, sense of self-worth, and connection to other people. Those who have been looking for work for six months or longer are more than three times as likely to become depressed as those who are employed in steady jobs. Feelings of shame, embarrassment, and strains in family relations are common.

Many people feel it's their fault if they cannot find a job. Why? Meaningful work is a human right. It is society's duty to provide an honest, meaningful job with an ample wage for each person who wants it. We should fight to demand jobs for all.

Prout's Vision: Cooperatives

Throughout the twentieth century and until today, cooperatives have been mostly invisible, ignored by most economists, the mass media and political leaders who are more concerned with power, fame and control. Yet more than one billion people, a sixth of our global population, are members of co-ops. The world's largest non-governmental organization is the International Cooperative Alliance (ICA), representing 246 national and global organizations.

The ICA defines co-ops thus: "A cooperative is an autonomous association of persons united voluntarily to meet their common economic, social, and cultural needs and aspirations through a jointly-owned and democratically-controlled enterprise."

Co-ops employ almost 10 percent of all of the world's employed people. In 156 countries, at least 280 million people are employed in or within the scope of co-ops. This is much more than the 80 million employed by multinational corporations (ICA 2018).

In Europe, there are at least 25,000 worker co-ops in Italy, about 17,000 (employing some 210,000 people) in Spain, 2,600 (employing 51,000 people) in France and about 500 to 600 in the UK (Pérotin 2016).

Cooperatives are also more likely to succeed than privately-owned enterprises. In the United States, 60 to 80 percent of companies fail in their first year, while only 10 percent of co-ops fail during that period. After five years, only three to five percent of new U.S. corporations are still in business, while nearly 90 percent of co-ops remain viable (World Council of Credit Unions 2003).

According to Prout, it is a basic right of workers in an economic democracy to own and manage their enterprises through collective management. These will produce the minimum necessities and most other products and services. Co-ops form the largest sector of a Prout economy. Smaller satellite co-ops can serve larger co-ops. For example, an automotive co-op could produce parts that are then shipped to nearby car manufacturing plants for final assembly.

There are three requirements for co-ops to succeed. The first is honest, trustworthy management. A high degree of integrity is vital to the firm's effectiveness. The second requirement is strict and transparent accounting to build trust among the co-op members and the community. The third requirement is for the local public to accept the cooperative system. This requires public education and constant promotion to create integrated networks of community co-ops.

Global capitalism, which wipes out local businesses around the world, also puts unfair pressure on co-ops. Decentralized economic democracy, however, ensures that each person in the community has a job and a voice in the decision-making process.

A cooperative market economy has many benefits: it keeps consumer prices low, decreases inflation, ensures low prices for raw materials, aids in the fair distribution of wealth, fosters closer ties among people, and builds community spirit.

Worker Cooperatives

Thriving co-ops grow from the energy and commitment of local people. The basis of the cooperative system lies in "coordinated cooperation," in which free human beings with equal rights and mutual respect work together to fulfill a common need, for their mutual benefit.

Co-ops differ from both traditional private enterprises and socialist communes formed through forced collectivization. Both of these systems are run through "subordinated cooperation," in which managers supervise and give orders to the workers. Co-ops, on the other hand, combine economic and social goals, spreading wealth and power to each member equally.

Co-ops hold a competitive advantage over both private and public enterprises because members have a personal interest in their co-op's success. The members own the co-op, so are more likely to buy its goods and use its services. Shares in co-ops are not publicly traded because the members own the shares. They themselves decide how to spend the co-op's profits.

Today many co-ops in capitalist countries involve pooling investment money and then sharing the profit. In Prout, only cooperative banks and consumer co-ops function like this. In all other co-ops, each member actively works for the project. This leads to a better working climate and enhanced productivity. In such co-ops, labor employs capital instead of the reverse. With labor at the helm and no longer subject to the dictates of capital, a sense of self-worth is restored to people and the community is strengthened.

Also in contrast to capitalism, co-op productivity is measured not only in terms of output and income, but also in terms of job security and happiness.

How Worker Cooperatives Function

Membership in a worker co-op is open only to those who work there. New workers are hired on a trial basis before they become full members. The control of the firm and the right to any residual assets and profits are based on the work of members rather than the value of capital or property holdings.

Control rests on the principle of one member, one vote, and not on the number of shares or amount of a person's investment in the co-op. If non-worker shareholders were allowed to become members, it would start conflicts of interest that could dilute the worker incentive system. Financing can be accepted only if it does not have the power to influence decision-making.

The incentive system for pay and profit-sharing must be both fair and attractive, so that competent people will join. While some co-ops pay all workers the same, others reward workers' performances according to their skill and contribution, but within a minimum and maximum income range. The ratio between the lowest-paid and highest-paid workers is figured with regard to the time and place, but the difference will naturally decrease as the overall standard of living rises. Rewards may also be given in other forms that boost productivity and worker satisfaction, such as better equipment, education and training, putting more workers in a unit, and work-related travel grants.

In private enterprises, financial incentives are used to demand high standards of training. Yet in co-ops, even higher levels of resourcefulness, social skills, and discipline among workers are needed. The value of investing in constant worker training to foster social skills as well as business management expertise cannot be stressed too much. Each member should be urged to further his or her education, keep abreast of technological advances in the field, and to share knowledge with others. The members' ability to play bigger roles in the venture will increase, and along with it, their self-esteem. In this way, cooperation and working conditions will improve for everyone.

Sharing of cooperative values and the sincere attempt to practice them allows people to integrate their social and economic lives with their beliefs. This can lead to a deeper sense of worker satisfaction, loyalty, and commitment to economic democracy.

The degree of collective decision-making depends on the size of the co-op. In small collectives, all members jointly make key decisions. Larger co-ops elect boards to make policy decisions. Boards select a manager who is a member of the co-op to be in charge of day-to-day operations. Each co-op, according to the realities of its business, must decide which decisions the manager, the board, and the entire membership respectively will make. Guidelines are based on other co-ops' experience.

Coordinated cooperation requires members and managers to have mutual respect and trust for one another. It is important to teach cooperative ethics to workers so that they can participate in and manage their firms. Where co-ops have been most successful, the managers are also teachers, stirring in the workers an understanding of the co-op and how it functions.

The Mondragon Corporation is the largest federation of worker co-ops based in the Basque region of Spain. It has more than 80,000 co-op worker-members. Their model of collective ownership relies on a balance of incentives. The innovative system of internal capital accounts spreads gains or losses in the net worth of the co-op to individual workers' accounts. The co-op restricts workers from taking out their balances at will, so that it can use the assets for reinvestment in the co-op. Interest is paid annually on each account. The balances on each member's account are paid out after a designated period of time, such as five years, or when a worker leaves the co-op.

Without good leadership and a wise cooperative structure, workers sometimes make poor decisions. For example, in the Vakhrusheva Coal Mine in the Khabarovsk Region of the Russian Far East, workers preferred instant dividends, high wages and access to imported goods as opposed to reinvesting their profits back into the development and long-term future of the co-op. Today this mine is being worked by a privately-owned company (Perkins).

Co-ops provide greater job security than do private enterprises, which are not answerable to the community and whose boards might choose to relocate to where wages are lower. Co-ops deem labor as a fixed rather than a variable cost over the short run. This means that workers are not immediately laid off if production is cut back. Viable alternatives to layoffs include cutting the work hours of all members, starting new lines of production or services, retraining workers, and transferring members to other co-ops.

A Supportive Infrastructure

It is difficult in a capitalist economy for a co-op to survive as an isolated enterprise. As Sarkar has noted, sincere acceptance of the cooperative system by the public is a requirement for success.

The vast majority of co-ops are fairly small. The only way they can afford certain services is through mutual support. Together, several co-ops may form a supportive infrastructure. This framework includes financing, technical and management assistance, joint marketing, joint purchasing of supplies and services, research and development of new products, cooperative education and training, and lobbying and public relations services. When co-ops have access to these types of support, they often outperform conventional private firms.

Access to funding from an allied credit union or bank is crucial to success. In the Mondragón group of co-ops, the Caja Laboral Cooperative Bank has provided the capital financing needed to grow and overcome many difficulties. It has 2,261 member-employees and generates annual revenue in excess of €330 million (Bloomberg 2018). The Stiga independent consulting report for 2009 rated Caja Laboral first among 105 financial institutions in Spain in terms of excellence of service (Mondragon Corporation Annual Report 2009).

Credit unions are cooperative banks, owned and democratically-managed by their members, which give loans at lower interest rates than commercial banks. Today there are 68,000 credit unions in 109 countries that serve 235 million people with $1.7 trillion in assets (World Council of Credit Unions 2016).

There are several reasons why credit unions are more successful than corporate banks. First, because they are legally registered as not-for-profit co-ops, earnings are not given away to stockholder investors. Second, credit unions do not speculate with their money on risky financial investments. Third, credit unions in the United States have been exempt from taxes since 1937, because they are member-owned, democratically operated, with the specific mission of meeting the credit and savings needs of consumers of modest means. Fourth, the members of the board of directors of each credit union are volunteers. Finally, credit unions are people helping people, working hard through education and community service to benefit everyone.

Worker and community takeovers of failed capitalist ventures have great potential. Argentina has the largest number of these takeovers; in response to the country's 2001 economic crisis, workers occupied bankrupt factories and collectively managed them. Called the Fábricas Recuperadas Movement, which means "reclaimed or recovered factories," this tactic expanded to other enterprises, such as the Hotel Bauen in Buenos Aires. The communities came out to defend these initiatives whenever the police tried to evict the workers.

The reclaimed businesses are run cooperatively, with key management decisions taken democratically by a general assembly of the workers. In most of these ventures, all workers receive the same wage. By 2016, about 16,000 Argentine workers were running 367 recovered businesses. In the first year since conservative president Mauricio Macri took office in December 2015, six recovered enterprises have failed. In Brazil in 2005, there were a total of 174 enterprises that had been taken over and were being managed by the workers as part of the solidarity economy (Juvenal 2006).

The benefits of worker-management include a higher level of loyalty and commitment by the workers, greater support from the community and less financial responsibility and stress on the shoulders of a single owner or CEO. The greatest obstacles faced are sometimes internal disputes and often problems getting credit for operations, because commercial banks are wary of lending to new cooperatively-managed enterprises, especially those with a history of financial troubles. In Argentina, recovered factories found it easier to join forces with other worker-managed enterprises to reach a critical size and power, which enabled them to negotiate successfully with the banks.

Co-ops have great potential to expand economic opportunity and wealth building for poor communities. In 2008 a group of community organizers in mainly African-American neighborhoods of Cleveland, Ohio, started the Evergreen Cooperative Initiative to create jobs and wealth building through a network of ecologically-friendly, community-based co-ops. In an area known as Greater University Circle where 43,000 residents have a median household income below $18,500 and where over 25 percent of the working population is unemployed, they used the Mondragón Cooperative Experience as a model to create a network of worker-owned enterprises. A non-profit corporation ties them together, with a revolving fund so that 10 percent of the income produced is used to start new co-ops (Wang 2011).

The Green City Growers Co-op is a year-round, hydroponic food production greenhouse. On just two hectares of land (5.5 acres), 40 employee-owners produce three million heads of healthy, organic lettuce and 300,000 pounds of herbs each year for local markets. The Evergreen Cooperative Laundry is an industrial-scale, high-tech laundry with more than 150 workers that uses only a third of the water and heat of traditional laundries to service the hospitals and the nursing homes in the area (Democracy Collaborative 2018). Ohio Cooperative Solar employs workers who "face barriers to employment" to install solar panels on Cleveland-area institutional, governmental, and commercial buildings. The enterprise became profitable within its first five months in operation; in the off-season the co-op helps weatherize low-income housing in the area. These co-ops focus on economic inclusion and building a local economy from the ground up (Wang 2011).

Co-ops benefit the community at large by creating jobs, retaining wealth, and by increasing social connections among the local people. The practice of economic democracy in co-ops raises awareness of democratic issues in the wider community.

Co-ops, much more than corporations, closely reflect the lives and thoughts of the member-owners. If the common interests of the members and the interests of the co-op move apart, the co-op dies.

Community Benefits

Full employment is possible by starting co-ops. This is especially crucial for women, who have been exploited by men throughout history because they were not economically independent. Jobless people everywhere can create co-ops that will earn them a decent income.

Co-ops benefit a community in many ways. They bring people together, encourage them to use their diverse skills and talents, and provide them with an opportunity to develop new capabilities. They strengthen the community by creating a sense of belonging, fostering close relationships among different types of people, and empowering people to make decisions to develop their community.

On an economic level, co-ops foster regional economic self-reliance and independence from outside control, empowering local people. They create employment, circulate money within the community, and offer a wide range of goods and services. Because co-ops are owned by the members themselves, profits stay in the local area. Co-ops thus increase the wealth and build the strength of the community.

In essence, successful cooperatives transform a community by establishing economic democracy. Co-ops are the businesses of the future. With global capitalism fatally ill, starting co-ops makes a lot of sense.

Activist Tools: How to Start a Successful Cooperative

In 1844, in the mill town of Rochdale near Manchester, England, 26 poor workers started the modern cooperative movement with a food co-op. Here are five principles as to how the lives of ordinary people could be improved:

1. **Start with the most essential products**: When the first cooperative shop opened in Rochdale, there were only four items for sale: flour, butter, sugar, and oatmeal. As the business grew, they gradually added other foods, books, and magazines.

2. **Produce and sell things within your own community**: This means making things that low-income people need and use. Consider basic foods, furniture, shoes, a taxi service, housing, and banking services.

3. **Allow people of all religious or political views**: The co-operators agreed to let people discuss any question at their meetings, but the organization itself would be neutral.

4. **Use some resources for education**: From the very start, the pioneers put part of their profits into an educational fund. In Rochdale, the first co-op started a library, while the Mondragón group of co-ops, which began in Spain about 100 years later, started with a technical engineering school.

5. **Share the profits**: Members of the co-op paid in a weekly sum of two pence, which later rose to three. However, these payments made them the owners of the shop and they received money back, five percent interest on the money plus their share of any profit the shop made.

Laws concerning co-ops are different in every country. In fact, some laws were written to hinder and block co-ops. Those who wish to start a co-op should first consult their national association of cooperatives and visit successful co-ops. It would be ideal to visit those which operate in the same sector, to learn as much as possible from the experience of others. These experienced co-op workers can also advise about psychological ways to win the support of the local people.

Here are suggestions on how to start a successful co-op:

1. Fulfill a need. People have to come together in order to fulfill a real need in the community. No matter how good the idea, if there is not a community need, the enterprise will not succeed.

2. Start a founding group. A few committed people have to take on the duty to develop the initial idea through to inception. Usually, however, one person will need to provide the leadership.

3. Commit to a vision. Commit to the ideals and values implicit in co-ops, and try to ensure that both the members and the management are honest, dedicated and competent.

4. Conduct a feasibility study. Objectively evaluate the perceived need, and decide if the proposed venture can fulfill that need by doing a feasibility study.

5. Set out clear aims and objectives. The members of each enterprise must formulate clear aims and objectives through consensus. These will help direct everything from the founding group's initial focus to promotional strategies in the years to come.

6. Create a sound business plan. Since the venture will require capital, members will have to manage co-op finances efficiently, and make effective decisions about loan repayments and profit sharing.

7. Ensure the support and involvement of the members. The members own the enterprise—at every step their support and involvement are essential.

8. Establish a location. Secure adequate premises for the venture, in the best possible location in the community.

9. Get skilled management. From within the community, bring into the venture people who have the needed management, business, financial, legal, and accounting skills.

10. Continue education and training. Ideally, the members will have the skills—chiefly the communication and interpersonal skills—needed to run the venture successfully. If not, they will either have to develop such skills or bring in new members who have them.

Activities

Do as many as you can:

What is the official unemployment level as defined by the government? What is the real unemployment level? How many people are unemployed? Are some demographic groups experiencing more unemployment than others?

Interview an unemployed person. How long have they been without a job? How do they survive? How do they feel about being unemployed?

Visit a co-op and interview one of the workers. Ask about their history, the problems they face, the mistakes they have made, and their successes. Ask how many workers are members, how much they are paid, and any other monetary, social, and personal benefits they receive.

Contact the national association of co-ops in your country. What is the total number of co-ops in your country? How many people are members of co-ops? What percentage of the population? Over time, is this percentage increasing or decreasing? Are the laws relating to co-ops favorable? Do co-ops receive tax breaks or other support from the government?

Further Readings

Alldred, Sarah. 2013. "Co-operatives Can Play a Key Role in Development." *The Guardian*, July 6, 2013.

Cooperative Development Institute. "Co-op 101: A Guide to Starting a Cooperative." The Northeast Center for Cooperative Business.

Kwakyewah, Cynthia. 2016. "Rethinking the Role of Cooperatives in African Development." *Inquiries Journal*, Vol. 8 No. 6, 1-2.

Pérotin, Virginie. 2016. "What Do We Really Know About Worker Co-operatives?" *Co-operatives UK*, September 2, 2016.

Thompson, Derek. 2015. "A World Without Work." *The Atlantic*, July/August 2015.

Further Viewings

Brodsky, Howard. 2017. "Cooperatives Build a Better World 2017." May 24, 2017. 30 minutes.

"Defying the Crisis - The Spanish Collective Mondragón." German Public Television, January 25, 2012. 5 minutes.

"Mondragon Corporation." 2014. 15 minutes.

Okuk, Niki. 2016. "When Workers Own Companies, the Economy is More Resilient." TEDxCrenshaw. October 2016, 12 minutes.

Veysey, Graham. 2010. "The Cleveland Model" Evergreen Cooperative Network. May 13, 2010. 6 minutes.

References

Bloomberg. 2018. "Company Overview of Caja Laboral Popular Coop. de Crédito."

Democracy Collaborative. 2018. "Evergreen Cooperative Laundry Expands to Second Plant, More than Tripling Its Workforce." May 10, 2018.

Elejalde-Ruiz, Alexia. 2018. "Unemployment Rate for Chicago's Black Youth Improves: Report." *Chicago Tribune*, May 12, 2018.

International Cooperative Alliance. 2018. "Facts and Figures."

Juvenal, Thais Linhares. 2006. "Empresas Recuperadas por Trabalhadores em Regime de Autogestão: Reflexões à Luz do Caso Brasileiro." *Revista do BNDES*, Rio De Janeiro, V. 13, N. 26, December 2006. p. 115-138.

Mondragon Corporation 2009 Annual Report.

Perkins, A. "On the Transition from State Planning to a Cooperative System of Production in the Former Soviet Union." Unpublished paper.

Re-Member, Inc. 2018. "Pine Ridge Indian Reservation"

Wang, Elaine and Nathaly Agosto Filión. 2011. "Case Study: Cleveland, OH: The Cleveland Evergreen Cooperatives" in *Sustainable Economic Development: A Resource Guide for Local Leaders*. Denver, CO: Institute for Sustainable Communities, pp. 30-36.

World Council of Credit Unions. 2003. "Statistical Data: United States Credit Union Statistics, 1939-2002."

— 2016. "Statistical Report."

MODULE 8: FOOD FOR ALL

Check Your Understanding

At the end of this module, you should be able to explain the following concepts:
How many people in the world are malnourished?
Why is there hunger in the world?
What crisis is agriculture facing?
What are the benefits and defects of farm subsidies?
What are the seven principles of food sovereignty?
What is the goal of Prout's "agrarian revolution?"
What are sustainable farming practices?
What are the benefits of agricultural cooperatives?
Can organic farming feed the world?
What are the problems with a meat-based diet?
What are permaculture, ecovillages, and Transition Towns?
What is the value of capturing media attention?

The Social Reality: Hunger

Some 815 million people in the world do not have enough food to lead a healthy active life. That's about one in nine people on earth.

Ninety-eight percent of those who suffer from hunger live in developing countries: 553 million live in the Asian and Pacific regions; 227 million live in Sub-Saharan Africa; and 47 million live in Latin America and the Caribbean. India has the highest population of hungry people. In 2014, over 190.7 million people were undernourished there.

Approximately nine million people die of hunger each year; 3.1 million of them are children. Forty percent of preschool-age children are estimated to be anemic because of iron deficiency. It is estimated that 250 to 500 thousand children go blind from Vitamin A deficiency every year.

Malnutrition causes stunting among children, a condition characterized by low height for a child's age. In 2017, it was estimated that 151 million children under five were stunted worldwide. Malnutrition also causes wasting, a condition characterized by low weight for a child's age. In 2017, it was estimated that 51 million children under five were wasted.

Great strides have been made toward ending world hunger. The Food and Agricultural Organization of the United Nations estimates that the total number of hungry people worldwide has been reduced by 216 million people since 1992 (all these statistics from Hunger Notes 2018).

Over 75 percent of the world's poorest people grow their own food. This causes widespread food insecurity in developing countries, as drought, climate change, and natural disasters can easily cut off a family's food supply (Turk 2017).

During the past 20 years, global food production has increased faster than the rate of global population growth. The world already produces enough to feed 10 billion people, more than our present population. But the people in extreme poverty cannot afford to buy it (Holt-Giménez et al. 2012). The simple reason that there is hunger is that feeding everyone and saving lives is not a universal priority.

Prout's Vision: A Crisis in Agriculture

For about 10,000 years, human societies have practiced many types of farming, shaping ecosystems to gain their basic needs: food, fiber for clothing, medicine, and raw materials for industry. Agriculture is a primary activity because it draws energy and resources from the environment. The greater the value of the agriculture, natural resources, and energy produced in any region, the greater is the potential of the rest of that economy.

During the last century, non-sustainable farming techniques have been launched on a large scale. Modern corporate farming is based on high inputs of chemical fertilizers, herbicides, and pesticides. Though high yields can be produced in the short-term, this gradually deteriorates the humus and structure of the soil. The burning of fossil fuels in agriculture and the large amounts of methane gas produced by breeding animals for slaughter in concentrated feedlots add to the global warming of the planet and to the poisoning of ground water. In the world's temperate climates, human agriculture has replaced 70 percent of grasslands, 50 percent of savannas, and 45 percent of temperate forests (Biello 2012).

Growing single crops is an over-simplification of nature. Large plantations of monocrops are, by their very nature, more at risk of harm due to pests and diseases than those planted with mixed crops. Farmers in the world apply 171 million metric tons of synthetic nitrogen fertilizer each year that poisons groundwater and pollutes nearby ecosystems. The runoff flows into rivers and promotes algal blooms that then die and, in their decay, suck all the oxygen out of surrounding waters, creating dead zones at the mouths of 405 of the world's rivers (Biello 2012).

In inorganic engineering, certain scientific principles are very effective. The laws of measurement, stress, balance, force, and counterforce allow us to produce valuable and reliable standard products according to a design—from structural steel and pre-stressed concrete to bricks and plywood.

In farming, though, this type of reductionist approach, which makes parts exactly the same, creates serious problems over time. Much of the fertility, range, and resilience of farmland depend precisely upon its biological complexity and lack of uniformity. Trying to standardize farming in monocultures endangers fertility.

Corporate agriculture also threatens biological diversity. In 1970 the United States passed the Plant Variety Protection Act to issue utility patents for living organisms and plants, and the U.S. Supreme Court has confirmed that. But local farmers the world over who have saved some seeds while rejecting others, thus changing plant species for thousands of years, are not protected or compensated.

The Union of Concerned Scientists and other major science organizations have found that some genetically engineered (GE) crops could be harmful to eat or harmful to the environment (Gurian-Sherman 2012). Currently, 64 countries around the world require labeling of genetically engineered (GE) food, including the 28 nations in the European Union, Russia, China, Brazil, India, Australia, Turkey, Japan, and South Africa. The United States does not (Just Label It Campaign 2018).

During the 1990s, the World Bank and the International Monetary Fund convinced India to remove trade barriers and to privatize export. The Indian government got rid of farm subsidies and opened their markets to multinational corporations. They urged farmers to switch from subsistence farming to export crops, especially cotton. Farmers bought genetically-modified seeds and pesticides from Monsanto, but then found themselves locked in by debt and at the mercy of global price swings. According to the Indian government, more than 300,000 Indian farmers have committed suicide from 1995 to 2018—one farmer every 35 minutes. Debt and economic hardship are blamed for these suicides (Sainath 2018).

Corporate farming is bankrupting small farmers and driving people off the land. In 1935 there were six million family farms in the United States where nearly 25 percent of the population lived. Today the number of family farms has decreased by more than two-thirds, from six million farms to only two million, and less than one percent of the US population works on the land (U.S. EPA 2015). This pattern occurs throughout the world, and as farmers lose their land and move to the city, many rural places where they lived become ghost towns.

Agricultural subsidies are direct payments to farmers by rich governments to supplement their income and to protect the country's food supply. Whereas this is a noble goal, in fact, agricultural subsidies go mostly to the biggest corporate farms, which overproduce and export the excess.

In 2010, the European Union spent €57 billion ($74 billion) on agricultural growth, of which €39 billion was spent on direct subsidies. Along with fisheries subsidies, this represents over 40 percent of the EU budget (Farmsubsidy.org). Yet the bulk of this money goes to very rich people. One in five of the biggest recipients of European farming subsidies in Britain are billionaires or millionaires. Greenpeace UK's policy director Dr. Doug Parr said, "It's simply indefensible that taxpayers' money is being used to bankroll huge subsidies going to billionaires, largely on the basis of how much land they own" (Beament 2017).

At this time the United States government pays farmers about $20 billion per year in direct subsidies that go to the largest producers of commodities like corn, soybeans, wheat, cotton, and rice. The largest 15 percent of farm businesses receive 85 percent of the subsidies, while producers of fruits and vegetables receive nothing. Once again, most of the money goes to big, rich landowners. According to the Government Accountability Office, between 2007 and 2011 the government paid some $3 million in subsidies to 2,300 farms where no crop of any sort was grown (Coburn 2015).

Farm subsidies lead to "international dumping," in which farmers "dump" food on foreign markets at prices lower than what it costs to produce it. Dumping causes developing countries to buy food cheaply from rich countries instead of from local farmers, which weakens their own agriculture and even bankrupts small growers, who lose their land.

Food Sovereignty

Via Campesina is a global peasant movement that unites the landless, rural women, peasants, farmers, small producers, and indigenous people in 81 countries. They work to defend local production of food and indigenous land rights. In 1996 this alliance coined the term "food sovereignty" to refer to the right of peoples to define their own food, agriculture, livestock, and fisheries systems, in direct conflict with agribusiness control and corporate manipulation for profit.

Via Campesina's seven principles of food sovereignty form a good base from which to achieve economic democracy and Prout's goal that every region should produce the food its people need:

1. Food is a Basic Human Right: Everyone must have access to enough safe, nutritious and culturally appropriate food to sustain a healthy life with full human dignity. Each nation should declare that ac-

cess to food is a constitutional right and ensure the growth of the primary sector to ensure the concrete realization of this basic right.

2. Agrarian Reform: A genuine agrarian reform is needed which gives landless and farming people—especially women—ownership and control of the land they work and returns territories to indigenous peoples. The right to land must be free of discrimination on the basis of gender, religion, race, social class, or belief systems. The land belongs to those who work it.

3. Protecting Natural Resources: Food Sovereignty entails the sustainable care and use of natural resources, chiefly land, water, seeds, and livestock breeds. The people who work the land must have the right to manage natural resources sustainably and to conserve biodiversity, free of restrictive intellectual property rights. This can only be done from a sound economic basis with security of tenure, healthy soils, and reduced use of agro-chemicals.

4. Reorganizing Food Trade: Food is first and foremost a source of nutrition and is of less value as an item of trade. National agricultural policies must make production for local use and food self-sufficiency the primary concern. Food imports must not displace local production nor depress prices.

5. Ending the Globalization of Hunger: Food Sovereignty is undermined by multilateral institutions and by speculative capital. The growing control of multinational corporations over agricultural policies has been aided by the economic policies of multilateral organizations such as the WTO, World Bank, and the IMF.

6. Social Peace: Everyone has the right to be free from violence. Food must not be used as a weapon. Growing levels of poverty and marginalization in the countryside, along with the growing oppression of indigenous peoples, most especially women and children, as well as all disenfranchised peoples, worsen cases of injustice and hopelessness. The ongoing displacement, forced urbanization, oppression, and increasing incidence of racism against smallholder farmers cannot be allowed.

7. Democratic Control: Small farmers must have direct input into creating agricultural policies at all levels. We all have the right to honest, accurate information and open and democratic decision-making. These rights form the basis of good governance, accountability, and equal participation in economic, political, and social life, free from all forms of discrimination. Rural women, chiefly, must be granted direct and active decision-making on food and rural issues.

Prout's Agrarian Revolution

One of Prout's goals is to restore *Pramá*—dynamic balance—in the environment. This concept is similar to what David Suzuki calls "the sacred balance" (Suzuki 1997). Prout advocates that we use Nature's gifts in a balanced and renewable way, while we preserve the planet's forests and other wild places and restore degraded areas. The difference between "utilizing" and "exploiting" the environment can be compared to "using" or "abusing" something.

Sarkar called for an "agrarian revolution," viewing agriculture as the most crucial sector of the economy. He stressed that every region should strive to produce the food its population needs. This simple idea of regional food supply is radically different from the corporate agriculture of today. Food in the United States travels on average between 1,500 and 2,500 miles (2500-4000 kilometers) from farm to table! The big winners of this are factory farms, agribusiness monopolies, giant supermarket chains, and long-distance shipping. The losers are farm communities and the Earth's climate (Worldwatch Institute).

Prout asserts that farming practices should be sustainable to preserve the planet's future. These techniques include organic farming, biological farming, permaculture, agro-forestry, holistic management, natural pest control, composting, mixed cropping, supplementary cropping, crop rotation, inter-cropping, and other similar practices.

Agricultural Cooperatives

Prout supports agricultural co-ops as the ideal form of farm management for many reasons. Cooperatives enable farmers to pool their resources, purchase inputs, and store and transport their market produce more easily. Most importantly, they eliminate the need for intermediaries—traders who buy produce very cheaply from the farmers and then sell it for a high price to city retailers. Instead, in a Prout economy, farmers' co-ops would sell directly to consumers' co-ops or to distribution co-ops, benefiting everyone. Finally, agricultural co-ops promote economic democracy, empowering farm families to decide their own future.

The co-ops of Prout are greatly different from the state-run "communes" of the former Soviet Union, China, and other communist countries which have, for the most part, been a failure. In these communes, very low rates of production often created drastic food shortages. By denying private ownership and incentives, they failed to create a sense of worker involvement. Central authorities issued plans and quotas, and the local people had no say over their work. Coercion, and sometimes violence, were used to run the commune system.

Prout does not support the seizing of farmland or forcing farmers to join co-ops. Traditional farmers have a strong bond with the land that has been held by their ancestors—some would rather die than lose it.

A major benefit of farm co-ops is the potential for the collective buying of farm equipment that is too expensive for most farmers. In addition, in countries where farmland is limited and population density is high, a good amount of land is wasted on borders and boundary fences that the co-op could use at once. By selling collectively, farmers will get higher prices for their produce.

Ideal Farming

Organic farming lessens environmental and human health impacts by avoiding the use of synthetic fertilizers, chemical pesticides, and hormones or antibiotic treatments for livestock. To compare organic farming with conventional agriculture using chemicals, environmental scientists at the University of California, Berkeley performed an analysis of 115 studies comparing conventional and organic methods. They found that organic agriculture delivers just five percent lower yield in rain-watered legume crops, such as alfalfa or beans, and in perennial crops, such as fruit trees. For major cereal crops and some vegetables, conventional methods delivered 19 percent more yield, mostly due to large doses of synthetic nitrogen fertilizer. However, when organic farmers apply best management practices, they perform better. Organic agriculture can feed the world (Ponisio 2015).

Prout promotes the practice of collecting seeds of different varieties and distributing them widely to preserve our planet's biodiversity.

Renewable energy sources can also be developed on agricultural co-ops through the use of bio-gas (produced in a tank of composting organic matter), solar power, and wind power.

Water conservation is a key issue in sustainability. Underground water reserves are crucial to a region's ecological balance; hence preference should be given to using surface water over well water for irrigation and other purposes. It is vital to reforest land to increase rainfall, and to construct many lakes and small ponds to capture rainwater. Planting certain trees that retain water in their roots along rivers and around lakes and ponds will help to prevent evaporation and maintain water levels.

A shift is needed in animal husbandry. Whereas domestic animals have played a huge role in agriculture for thousands of years—fertilizing the soil and turning grass into milk, for example—the present cattle, sheep and poultry industries are causing great ecological damage. Worldwide, about 70 billion farm animals are now raised for food each year. Two out of every three of these are being factory farmed, kept permanently in confined cages or pens. Farm animals consume half the world's grain (A Well-Fed World 2018).

It is not only cruel to raise animals for slaughter, it is inefficient, too. For each seven kilograms of plant protein, such as cereals, that is fed to livestock in factory farms, only one kilogram of protein on average is given back in the form of meat or other livestock products. The vast lands and huge amounts of water used to grow animal feed and to raise livestock could feed many more people if planted with grains, beans and other crops for human consumption (J.L.P. 2013).

Awareness is growing of the ill effects on health of eating a diet high in meat. Prout supports eating less meat for both health and ecological reasons.

Permaculture, Ecovillages, and Transition Towns

Three growing, progressive movements today for sustainable agriculture and sustainable communities are permaculture, ecovillages, and Transition Towns.

In Australia, David Holmgren and Bill Mollison coined the term 'permaculture' in 1978 to describe a system of agricultural and social design principles centered around simulating or directly utilizing the patterns and features observed in natural ecosystems. Permaculture includes ecological design, ecological engineering, environmental design and construction, and integrated water resources management (Mollison 1991).

Mollison has said: "Permaculture is a philosophy of working with, rather than against nature; of protracted and thoughtful observation rather than protracted and thoughtless labour; and of looking at plants and animals in all their functions, rather than treating any area as a single product system" (Mollison 1991).

The 12 principles of permaculture are: observe and interact, catch and store energy, obtain a yield, apply self regulation and accept feedback, use and value renewable resources and services, produce no waste, design from patterns to details, integrate rather than segregate, use small and slow solutions, use and value diversity, use edges and value the marginal, and creatively use and respond to change (Holmgren 2002).

Communes were intentional communities based on shared living that sprung up in many places in Europe and North and South America in the 1960s and 1970s. Most collapsed; some that survived into the 1980s focused on co-housing and ecology. In 1987 in Denmark, Ross and Hildur Jackson founded Gaia Trust as a charity to support sustainability projects around the world through grants and proactive initiatives. They in turn inspired Robert and Diane Gilman to co-author *Ecovillages and Sustainable Communities* (Blouin 2007).

Kosha Joubert, Executive Director of the Global Ecovillage Network, defined an 'ecovillage' as an "intentional, traditional, rural, or urban community that is consciously designed through locally owned, participatory processes in all four dimensions of sustainability (social, culture, ecology, and economy) to regenerate their social and natural environments" (Joubert 2015).

Most ecovillages range from a population of 50 to 150 individuals, although some are smaller or larger than that. The more than 500 members of the Findhorn community in Scotland hosted the first ecovillage conference in 1995. Today, there are over 10,000 self-identified ecovillages in over 70 countries on six continents (GEN 2018).

The Transition Network began in Totnes in southwest England in 2005 by permaculture designer Rob Hopkins, Peter Lipman, and Ben Brangwyn. The purpose is for communities to increase their self-sufficiency and reduce the potential impacts of peak oil, climate destruction, and economic instability. They are reclaiming the economy, sparking entrepreneurship, reimagining work, reskilling themselves, and weaving webs of connection and support. Transition Towns have now spread to over 50 countries, in thousands of towns, villages, cities, universities, and schools. Communities address global challenges by starting local and crowd-sourcing solutions (Transition Network 2016).

Activist Tools: Capturing Media Attention

One of the most powerful means to raise consciousness of people locally and around the world is through the media: TV, radio, newspapers, magazines, and social media. Of course, all large, popular media outlets are owned and controlled by huge corporations, and so many of them may try to devalue and marginalize us. But through our solidarity, our actions and our words, we can use these moments in history to convey a radical and inspiring message to the people of the world.

There isn't any one sure-fire way to get your message out to the public. Instead try a multi-touch approach. Consider social media, websites, event calendars, email, direct mail, radio, TV, print media, and flyers. Here are four suggestions to help you get your message out to a wide target audience by utilizing social and mass media platforms effectively.

Choose a clear, fresh message. Decide what you are calling for and keep repeating it clearly and concisely. If you speak calmly and appeal to common understandings, radical ideas can appear not only sensible but even obvious. Start with an inspiring theme to engage your audience and keep it consistent throughout the event.

Plan it and share it. Start with a plan. Decide on your goals, your target audience and how to best reach them. Create key messaging to use in all communications.

Use Social Media. Ever since the 2010-11 Arab Spring Protests, organizing protests and events using social media has been the way to go. Around the world, more and more people are tuning into social media. In fact, in the United States, many newspapers have gone out of business, or now have only online versions (Shearer and Gottfried 2017).

Make it easy for folks to share on your website and link all your social media.

Twitter: Create a hashtag for the event and ask folks to use it to tweet about the event.

Facebook: Make a Facebook Event Page. Invite your friends to 'like' the page and share it.

YouTube: Create a short video to promote your event and upload it to YouTube or Flickr.

LinkedIn: Promote on your own LinkedIn network by sharing an update with a link to your event page.

Use Mass Media:

Interviews: Use your slogan or message as much as possible. The average "sound bite" that TV or radio uses is only seven seconds long, and the print media usually publishes no more than two or three lines when quoting someone. Memorize three sound bites (with backup information) and write them down. If possible, introduce yourself and smile. Ask the journalist's name and media outlet if they didn't identify themselves. Never lie. Avoid profanities, because they will only give people an excuse not to listen to your message.

Be careful about questions that belittle you and your cause. For example, "Are you disappointed with the low turnout today?" In that case, follow this "ABC":

Acknowledge the question,

Bridge away from it, and

Communicate your message.

So to the above question you might reply, "I'm inspired, because each person here stands for hundreds of people in the so-called Third World who are being impoverished and exploited by undemocratic, unaccountable institutions such as the IMF, WTO, and World Bank for the benefit of transnational corporations and the super rich."

Practice! Even people who speak all the time practice. Know the opposing points and decide the best reply to each one.

If you slip up, ask the reporter to start again (unless it's live). If you need more time to think, ask the reporter to repeat the question, or ask a clarifying question, or simply pause and think before answering. If you don't know an answer to a question, don't force it. Try to return to your message. If it's an interview for print media, tell the reporter you'll track down the answer later and call them back.

An interview is never over even if the tape stops rolling. Everything you say to a journalist is on the record.

Print Media: Newspaper reporters, who often cover beats (issue areas), are usually more likely to engage in a detailed discussion of your issue and want more precise answers to their questions than do broadcast journalists. Explain your position fully, and stress the key points you want to appear in the paper.

Radio: Ask how long the interview will last. Rehearse your message and any events or web pages you want to announce before the interview and practice. Have a friend ask you questions and tape your responses. Use humor, personal stories, and concrete messages. You can use notes, but don't read. Warm up your voice by talking for a few minutes before. Speak clearly, but not too slowly.

Most radio interviews are conducted by phone, so find a quiet place for the call.

Don't answer questions with a simple 'yes' or 'no.' Explain your position and have an exchange with the host. Repeat your message more than once, because listeners may tune in late.

Vary your voice, and avoid "ah" and "um." Try to sound as if you are speaking to a friend.

Ask supporters to call in while you're on the show. Ask someone to tape the show so you can listen to it later. If the station will post the interview on their website, post the link on your social media.

Television: Dress well to make an impression. Ask if the show will be taped and edited, or broadcast live. Every blink, 'uh,' and twitch is magnified on camera. Look at the reporter or the camera operator. Don't look into the camera unless you are talking from the field to an anchor back at the studio.

Give personal and moving examples. Refer to concrete images. Keep your answers brief and stick to your key points. The more tape they have, the less control you have over what they put on the air.

Finally, thank the journalist, ask for his or her card, and ask when the story will be run.

Media Event: This is an activity intended to generate news coverage. They often involve colorful visuals, playful stunts, props, etc. The more of the following traits it has, the more likely your media event will get covered: novelty, conflict, new data that shows a trend, simplicity, humor, a prominent figure, action, bright props and images, local impact, holidays, or anniversaries.

Build your media event site, speakers, and visuals around your message and slogan. Make it fun. Don't be afraid to employ stunts. The media prefer exciting current events to long range things.

Consider timing. Is your event competing with other things? It is best to stage an event Monday through Thursday, 10 A.M. through 2 P.M.

Choose an effective location that is unique and convenient, because reporters are busy and won't travel far for an event. Protesting outside a company office is usually less effective than at the company's annual meeting, where business journalists may be present.

Check with the local police department if you need a permit. If your event is outdoors, have a backup location in case of bad weather.

Display a large banner or sign with your organization's logo. Arrange to have good photographers take pictures of your event. The event should last 15 to 45 minutes.

Pass out handouts about your issue and organization at the event. Have spokespersons ready to be interviewed.

Send your report of the event to all reporters who did not attend.

Press Release: This informs journalists about your event, report, or issue. It should include all the information a reporter needs to write their piece. Write the press release as the news story *you* would want to see written. Type your release on your organization's letterhead; send it out at least three weeks before the event. Newspapers have deadlines; you need to research and be sure to get the release in well before the deadline.

In the top left corner, type "For Immediate Release," and just below that, type the date. In the top right corner, type names and phone numbers of two contacts that can answer questions and are easily reached by phone.

Your headline will make or break a news release. Include the most important content in the headline, and make it punchy. Keep the headline short and use a large font.

Important content should jump off the page, because most reporters will spend at most 30 seconds looking at a release. Spend 75 percent of your time writing the headline and the first paragraph. Use the inverted pyramid style of news writing, that is, include the most newsworthy content—who, what, when, where, and why— in the first paragraph, other key details in the second paragraph, then work your way down with more general and background information.

Keep sentences and paragraphs short, with only one, two, or at most three sentences per paragraph. Include a colorful quote from a spokesperson in the second or third paragraph. Include a short summary of your organization in the last paragraph.

Mention "Photo Opportunity" if there is one, and send a copy of the release to the photo desk.

Type MORE at the end of page 1 if your release is two pages, and repeat the contact phone numbers and short headline in the upper-right hand corner of subsequent pages.

If your release announces an event, send it to the daybooks. Daybooks are event calendars posted by wire services and larger news outlets in large cities that list each day's area news events. Basic details are given for each event, including: location, time, speaker, and contact person. Editors use daybooks to assign reporters and photographers each morning to events they've chosen to cover. (Find out whether your city has one by calling the newsroom of your largest local newspaper).

Always make follow up calls after you send the release. Journalists insist that it is OK to call repeatedly, as long as you are polite each time. If your release announces an event, make the calls the morning before your event is scheduled. Have a copy of the release ready to be faxed or emailed when you make the calls, because they may have lost or misplaced the earlier one.

Media Advisory: This is sent to news outlets three to five working days before an upcoming event to alert journalists. It gives a short description of the event and the issue and answers who, what, where, when and why. The headline and format are the same as a press release, except that in the top left corner, type "Media Advisory."

Describe how your event will look visually, for example, "Citizens will carry large placards and life-size puppets to the Governor's Mansion to protest the latest cut in education funding." List the speakers at your event.

Opinion Piece: An op-ed is a personal opinion essay which is typically published opposite the editorial page. They help legitimize your cause and you as an informed spokesperson for it.

Write a catchy first paragraph using a personal story or concrete example. Clearly state your specific point of view. Aim for 700 to 750 words and double space. Write in the active voice with two-to-three-sentence paragraphs. Avoid jargon and academic language. Write in a personal, storytelling way. Use humor, if possible.

Give the op-ed a short title. Find a local angle for local papers; write more broadly for a national paper.

Put your name, phone, and address in the top left-hand corner. Type the number of words in the top right-hand corner.

Before you send it, call and pitch the piece to the editor of the op-ed page to see if there is any interest. Call early in the week and early in the day.

Pitching Your Story: In the past, telephone calls were the most effective way to communicate with reporters. Today many reporters prefer email and texts. Reporters are overloaded with paper, so chances are they never saw your release or advisory.

Target your reporters. Contact reporters who cover your issue, and reporters you have a relationship with. If you have to make a cold call, ask the general assignment editor or producer who you should speak to.

Find a hook for your story. Show the reporter how your story is hot, significant, timely, controversial, or how it impacts a lot of readers.

Keep the pitch short and punchy. Reporters don't have time for long pitch calls, so tell the essential information (who, what, where, when, and why) in the first 90 seconds. Then ask if they received your release or advisory.

Be enthusiastic and helpful. If you're not excited about your story, why should the reporter be?

Never lie to a reporter. They may not like what you have to say, but if you're honest, they must respect you.

Be considerate of deadlines. Pitch calls are best made in the mid morning (9:30 to noon). If you sense a reporter is rushed or impatient, ask them if they are on deadline and offer to call back.

Only pitch one reporter per outlet. If you do talk to more than one person, make sure the other reporter knows that you've talked with someone else.

Close the deal. Ask the reporter if they are interested or if they are coming to the event. Most will not commit over the phone but they will think about it.

Offer to send them a report right after the event if they cannot attend.

Pitch calls can be frustrating when reporters don't bite. But remember that every phone call keeps your issue and organization on their radar screen, and is an important step in building an on-going professional relationship with reporters.

Press Conference: This is a scheduled meeting to release new information about an issue, announce a further event, or respond to breaking news.

Press conferences seldom get much coverage from media, so it is usually better to stage a media event, or call reporters and email them information.

Hold the conference outside, if possible, but with an indoor backup in case of bad weather.

Choose a space that fits your audience. Don't use a room for 50 if you only expect eight, because it will appear as though the public is not interested in your issue. Ask your supporters to fill empty seats so the event looks well attended for the reporters and TV cameras.

Practice the press conference in advance, including questions.

Place your group's logo in front of the podium. Provide refreshments.

Assign someone to greet reporters, hand each one a press kit, and ask them to sign in.

Use at most four speakers, the most important ones first, with each one talking a maximum of five minutes, and give ten minutes at the end for questions. Speakers should dress in formal clothes unless they are in uniforms or costumes. Create props for your speakers to hold, or large charts and diagrams that they can point to.

Start and end on time. Reporters can interview speakers after the event if they want.

Unexpected Media Calls: This means the journalists know who you are and are coming to you as an expert. Ask what the reporter needs. Do they want a quote or background information? If you are not sure how to respond, simply jot down the question, verify the reporter's deadline, and assure them that you will return the call before that time.

Don't ignore the media. Neglected reporters have a long memory. Try to answer the reporter's questions as quickly and completely as possible.

Nothing is ever off the record. Don't say anything you wouldn't want to see in print.

Activities

Do as many as you can:

Interview local farmers. Ask them about their successes and challenges. Ask them what their biggest problems are.

Find out what percentage of your country's population works in agriculture, industry, and services? What would be the effect if your economy became more balanced?

Visit a cooperative farm or a Community Supported Agriculture (C.S.A.) farm.

Survey your family and friends. How many of them grow food in a garden? Ask those who do grow their own food, how it makes them feel.

Organize a media event.

Further Readings

Biello, David. 2012. "Will Organic Food Fail to Feed the World?" *Scientific American*, April 25, 2012.

Duhamel, Philippe. 2005. "Lessons from a Successful Media Campaign."

Feenstra, Gail, Chuck Ingels, and David Campbell. "What is Sustainable Agriculture?" University of California at Davis, Agricultural Sustainability Institute.

Ghobadi, Shahla. 2018. "Going Viral: What Social Media Activists Need to Know." *The Conversation*, July 17, 2018.

Hunger Notes. 2018. "2018 World Hunger and Poverty Facts and Statistics."

Further Viewings

Black, Simon. 2018. "DIY Activism: Getting Media Coverage." Greenpeace Australia Pacific. February 18, 2018. 3 minutes.

Foley, Jonathan. 2010. "The Other Inconvenient Truth." TEDxTC. October 2010. 18 minutes.

Holmgren, David. 2015. "Permaculture and Reading Landscape." Living in the Future. September 10, 2015. 16 minutes.

"Organic Sustainable Farming is the Future of Agriculture — The Future of Food." Happen Films. May 21, 2017. 6 minutes.

"The Paradox of Hunger in the World." June 5, 2013. 8 minutes.

References

Beament, Emily. 2017. "EU Farming Subsidies: One in Five Biggest Recipients are Billionaires and Millionaires on the UK Rich List. *Independent,* June 30, 2017.

Biello, David. 2012. "Will Organic Food Fail to Feed the World?" *Scientific American,* April 25, 2012.

Blouin, Michael. 2007. "The Urban Ecovillage Experiment: The Stories of Six Communities that Hoped to Change the World."

Coburn, Tom. 2015. "Milking Taxpayers." *The Economist,* February 12, 2015.

Farmsubsidy.org

Global Ecovillage Network. 2018. "About GEN."

Gurian-Sherman, Doug. 2012. "Is the Long-Term Safety of Genetically Engineered Food Settled? Not by a Long Shot." Union of Concerned Scientists. November 15, 2012.

Halley, Lori. 2013. "5 Tips for Getting Your Event Message Out." NTen. February 15, 2013.

Holmgren, David. 2002. *Permaculture: Principles and Pathways Beyond Sustainability*. Holmgren Design Services.

Holt-Giménez, Eric, Annie Shattuck, Miguel Altieri, Hans Herren and Steve Gliessman. 2012. "We Already Grow Enough Food for 10 Billion People … and Still Can't End Hunger." *Journal of Sustainable Agriculture*, 36:6, pp. 595-598.

Hunger Notes. 2018. "2018 World Hunger and Poverty Facts and Statistics."

J.L.P. 2013. "Meat and Greens." *The Economist,* December 31, 2013.

Joubert, Kosha. 2015. "From Apartheid to Ecovillage." TEDXFindhorn June 1, 2015.

Just Label It Campaign. 2018. "Labeling Around the World."

Mollison, Bill. 1991. *Introduction to Permaculture*. Tasmania, Australia: Tagari.

Ponisio, Lauren, L.K. M'Gonigle, Kevi Mace, Jenny Palomino, Perry de Valpine, and Claire Kremen. 2015. "Diversification Practices Reduce Organic to Conventional Yield Gap." *Proceedings. Biological sciences / The Royal Society*. 282. 20141396. 10.1098/rspb.2014.1396.

Sainath, P. 2018. "A Long March of the Dispossessed to Delhi." *The Wire,* June 23, 2018.

Shearer, Elisa and Jeffrey Gottfied. 2017. "News Use Across Social Media Platforms 2017." Pew Research Center. September 7, 2017.

Suzuki, David. 1997. *The Sacred Balance*. Australia: Allen and Unwin.

Transition Network. 2016. "What is Transition?"

Turk, Chasen. 2017. "15 World Hunger Statistics." The Borgen Project. March.

U.S. Environmental Protection Agency. 2015. "Ag 101 Demographics."

A Well-Fed World. 2018. "Factory Farms."

World Bank. "3.2 Agricultural Inputs."

Worldwatch Institute. "Globetrotting Food Will Travel Farther Than Ever This Thanksgiving."

MODULE 9: IDEAL LEADERSHIP

Check Your Understanding

At the end of this module, you should be able to explain the following concepts:
Define incompetent, inefficient, and dangerous leaders.
How do sociology, Marxism, and Prout define social classes?
What are the positive and negative aspects of each of Prout's four classes?
What is the Social Cycle and how does it rotate?
What is a Shudra Revolution and who leads it?
What are the qualities of sadvipras?
What is the role of sadvipras?
What is the inner struggle of a sadvipra?
What is "emotional intelligence?"

The Social Reality: Dangerous Leaders

A position of leadership gives one an unusual degree of influence over others which can be either positive or negative. Studies in capitalist firms show that the actions of the leader account for up to 70 percent of how employees perceive their organization (Beck and Harter 2015).

Incompetent and inefficient leaders tend to cause their organizations to be incompetent and inefficient, wasting everyone's time. The Peter Principle is a management concept developed by Laurence J. Peter in 1969, which observes that people in a hierarchy tend to rise to their "level of incompetence." This means that an employee is promoted based on their success in previous jobs until they reach a level at which they are no longer competent. This happens because skills needed in one job do not necessarily transfer to another job (Peter and Hull 1969).

Besides those leaders who are incompetent or inefficient, some leaders are actually dangerous. We can spot dangerous leaders by comparing them to psychopaths, whom psychologists recognize as having a personality disorder of persistent antisocial behavior, impaired empathy and remorse, and bold, uninhibited, and egotistical traits. Psychopaths are usually charming, charismatic, and intelligent. They brim with self-confidence and independence, and exude sexual energy. They are also extremely self-absorbed, masterful liars, compassionless, often sadistic, and possess an insatiable appetite for power (Patrick, Fowles, and Krueger 2009).

That insatiable appetite for power means that psychopaths will go to any lengths to become leaders, whether it be of a criminal gang, or a nation.

Of course, not all bad leaders are psychopaths. But here are some traits that can harm organizations and people that they control:

Autocratic: they want control over everything. Overbearing and distrustful, they do not share information. They do not listen well, and do not recognize the achievements of others. Mistreating people creates high levels of stress, turnover, absenteeism, and burnout among those around them.

Narcissistic and vain: they often rely on contempt to make others feel like losers, so that they feel like winners. They will belittle the work of others or ridicule them at meetings. When they need something, they may threaten. People around them often doubt themselves.

Paranoid: they tend to be suspicious and mistrustful of others. Feeling in danger and easily insulted, they constantly look for signs and threats that validate their fears or biases. They tend to be guarded and have very constricted emotional lives. They bear grudges, and tend to interpret others' actions as hostile.

Prout's Vision: Classes Based on Social Psychology

Social classes are forms of 'social stratification.' Sociologists usually denote three main classifications: the upper class or elite, the middle class, and lower class. What mainly determines social class are a person's hereditary family, wealth, income, influence, power, educational attainment, and job prestige. In Latin America, for example, race and ethnicity have been and still are prime determinants of class, with white-skinned colonial elites claiming privilege, and the various mixed-race, indigenous, and African descendants having much less privilege. The same is true in North America.

In Marxist theory, only two main classes exist. First are the capitalists or bourgeoisie, who own the means of production and purchase the labor power of others. Second are the workers or proletariat, who only have their own labor power which they sell for a wage or salary. Marx believed that the members of each class share common economic interests, and they engage in collective action which advances their interests. In other words, the workers try to increase their wages and benefits, while the capitalists try to increase their profits and reduce their costs, including the wages and benefits of their workers.

P. R. Sarkar presents a radically different perspective on social classes. Basing his model on how humans relate to their natural and social environments, he identifies four basic types. In Sanskrit, these groups are known as *varnas*, or "mental colors." The concept of varnas is a valuable model to analyze class dynamics. Like archetypes, these classifications are useful to identify the powerful forces which impact societies. They are less useful for understanding individual psychology, where other complex factors apply.

This concept of varnas generates a model of social dynamics and historical analysis unique to Prout. The theory holds that, at any given time, a society is dominated by the psychology and administration of a particular varna. It further proposes that social change occurs in cycles. Together these ideas are referred to as the Theory of the Social Cycle, which describes the changes that take place in society as dominant values and power bases shift from one varna to the next in a cyclic manner.

The four varnas are: *shudras* (workers); *ksattriyas* (warriors); *vipras* (intellectuals); and *vaeshyas* (merchants).

Prout's theory of class differs from the caste system of India, which uses the same terms, but locks people into a rigid system of hierarchy and discrimination by birth. Sarkar strongly opposed the caste system. Instead, he viewed varna as a psychological outlook which manifests in a particular style of survival and growth in a given environment.

On an individual level, every person possesses a mixture of and potential for all the four varnas, although usually one psychology tends to be dominant. Through education, training, and social environment, a person can develop any of these tendencies, or even all four simultaneously. Each varna has both positive and negative qualities.

Shudra (Worker): Skilled tradespersons know how to work well, how to make things, and how to fix things. When you need a job done, you look for a worker who takes pride in their labor. Workers tend to support one another and often develop a keen spirit of trust and friendship. These people tend to work hard, and to enjoy mundane pleasures. Sports, drinking, good food, and television are common pastimes. The shudra mind seeks safety, security, and some creature comforts. Workers tend to be followers, not leaders. Of course, the shudras of today are much more developed than those of the past. Shudras live according to the trends of the dominant collective psychology. This class essentially reflects mass psychology.

In general, common people who have not been politicized and who have not entered a struggle for social justice, exhibit these traits. However, the mentality of working and unemployed people changes when their consciousness is raised, when they begin to fight for their rights and the rights of others. As their minds expand and they acquire new skills and viewpoints, their varna begins to shift.

Ksattriya (Warrior): The second varna is composed of those with a warrior bent, who bravely confront the environment with physical strength and fighting spirit. Such people who embrace challenge and struggle gravitate toward athletics and martial arts, the military, police, firefighting, seafaring, and rescue work. They strive for self-mastery through will, patience, and hard work. They are willing to take calculated risks to achieve a noble goal, and are ready to die to keep a promise or oath. Usually stoic, they give great importance to loyalty, honor, integrity, courtesy, discipline, and self-sacrifice for others, to protect the weak.

Yet on the negative side, they may also choose violent aggression, blind obedience, machismo, cruelty, and ruthless competition. They can be trained to kill, to torture, to commit war crimes and crimes against humanity. The Nazi and Japanese empires that committed crimes against humanity were ksattriya societies gone amok.

Vipra (Intellectual): Those with a developed intellect, who seek to impact society by virtue of their mind, make up this third class. Their positive qualities include critical thinking, curiosity, and skepticism. They can think independently, teach and share ideas, concepts, arguments, and explanations. Vipras push scientific, religious, and cultural boundaries, question assumptions, and do original, creative research. They can use their gifted minds to inspire and empower others, ideally developing humility, intuition, and wisdom.

But vipras can also allow their dark side to grow. Theoretical, impractical and irrelevant intellectuals can waste their time on projects that benefit no one. They can be arrogant, cynical, and argumentative. They can criticize, insult, and condemn opponents. Hiding their ugly nature through hypocrisy and clever lies, they may impose dogmas, fear, and inferiority complex in simple-minded people. Creating divisive rules and policies for their own selfish desires, they can manipulate, dominate, and verbally torture others.

Vaeshya (Merchants): The fourth varna or social class is that of the vaeshyas, a merchant class which excels in managing and accumulating resources. An entrepreneur is a risk taker and opportunity seeker who always looks for new ideas and money-making opportunities and then makes a plan to get them to market. Results-oriented, these people are efficient and effective, strategically organizing and managing large numbers of people to get tasks done. Imaginative, ambitious, and innovative, they are persistent and refuse to accept the idea that something is impossible. Creating wealth, they have the capacity to enrich communities and benefit thousands of people with creative products, services, and jobs.

Sadly, people with a merchant mindset can also be ruthless exploiters. Greedy to own everything, they can mercilessly bankrupt competitors. The craving for more wealth even propels some capitalists to exploit the markets of corruption, pornography, the sex trade, drugs, and organized crime.

History and the Social Cycle

The social cycle progresses in a natural sequence of historical eras from shudra (laborer) society to ksattriya (warrior), followed by vipra (intellectual), and then vaeshya (merchant). Later on, a new cycle begins. This cyclical view of history does not imply that society moves in circles, retracing its steps. Rather, the social cycle is like a spiral that gradually progresses toward greater human consciousness.

The launch of each era is dynamic on all levels: political, cultural, and economic. This occurs as new leaders arise and free people from the oppressive institutions of the old order. This optimistic trend peaks sooner or later as the new class tightens its control. Finally social decline occurs as the dominant class strives to carry on its power at the expense of the basic needs of the people. Social unrest builds.

From the time of the first human beings, who lived together in clans or tribes for mutual safety, shudras struggled to survive amid the dangerous forces of nature. Through clashes with the environment and inter-group conflicts over food and other resources, the human mind slowly became stronger and more complex. In this way, some humans developed confidence, bravery, and the capacity to rule and dominate over others as well as their environment. Thus the ksattriya psychology appeared.

These Stone Age warriors gradually won acceptance as symbols of the unity of the tribe in the true beginning of human society in its most basic form. Unity, discipline, and a sense of social responsibility slowly developed in these clans. The fight for prestige and supremacy raged between different clans during the Ksattriyan Era, and people developed strong feelings of loyalty and pride regarding their clan. The early ksattriya societies were matriarchal.

The golden era of the ksattriyas was one of expansion and conquests, dating from the prehistoric era through the great empires of ancient history until the end of the Roman Empire, the Chin Dynasty and the Indo-Aryan expansion. Ksattriyas greatly valued courage, honor, discipline and devotion to duty, making ksattriya societies well-organized and united.

In the struggle of warrior societies against one another, human intellect grew. The ingenuity of the vipras resulted in the first scientific advances. As armies became larger, superior weapons, strategy, and logistics became as decisive as strength and skill. Without sharp minds to devise tactics, victory in warfare became impossible. As cities and nations grew, skilled administrators became essential. Hence vipras gradually became the most valued assets of the ksattriya leaders.

Over time the intellectual ministers acquired more actual power than the warrior kings. At the same time, organized religion assumed the role formerly held by tribal shamans. The Hindu and Buddhist societies of Asia were vipra-led, as was the Catholic Church, which gained greater power than all the royalty of Europe. Islam swept across the Middle East, Northern Africa, and Asia. In Tibet, the monks and lamas assumed both political and religious power. With the coming of the Vipran Age the personal authority of the warrior kings became less important as social administration based on scriptures and laws developed. Through different social, religious, and scriptural injunctions, intellectuals in the roles of minister, priest, lawmaker, and adviser began to rule society and shape its growth.

In the vipra stage of the social cycle education and culture thrived. Human beings attained new heights of mental development and awareness. Cultural, religious, and governmental institutions grew during the golden age of the vipras. Science, art, and the other branches of knowledge flourished under these hosts. The early Buddhist ages of India, China, and Southeast Asia all illustrate this trend, as do the monastic centers of learning in the European Middle Ages. Some rulers, such as King Frederick the Great, were great patrons of science and learning.

In time, of course, the vipra class also became oppressive, focusing on their own material and social privileges. To keep control, they resorted to hypocrisy, injecting superstitions, dogmas, and psychic complexes into the minds of the other classes.

Gradually, their concern with comfort and privilege caused the vipras to obey the vaeshyas, who were building more and more wealth. In turn they developed the capacity to buy the vipras' land and to employ them in their service. In this way, the merchant class slowly grew in size and influence, infusing new dynamism into societies that had been suffering under a corrupt vipra class. The skillful and practical vaeshyas directed the great ocean voyages of discovery around the Earth and captured tremendous wealth.

When the conquistadors and colonizers first arrived in the Americas, Spain, Portugal, France, and England were in transition from vipra societies—led by a royal family, court ministers, and the Church—to a vaeshyan one. They employed the warrior class with their superior weapons to invade and colonize the world in an effort to extract resources, including slaves. Most indigenous tribes of the Americas and Africa that they came across were led by warriors (ksattriyas), though it is possible that a few were led by intellectual "shamans" (vipras). The vast fortunes that were made in the colonies and through slavery helped to establish the wealthy elites as the new power brokers.

In Latin America, Africa and elsewhere, European capitalists also urged priests and ministers to try to convert the people to Christianity. Wherever they were successful, inferiority complexes were imposed and the populations became more compliant. Leonardo Boff and others have argued that there have, in effect, always been two Catholic Churches in Latin America: one of the rich and one of the poor. The Catholic Church of the rich and the military has served the financial interests of capitalists.

As the merchants gained power, they created new financial, political, and social systems. Democratic movements led to the creation of the House of Commons in Great Britain, the American, French, and Haitian revolutions, and a slow increase in gender equality. Great advances in the arts and sciences were also inspired under the patronage of the merchant class.

Capitalists tend to view all things, even human beings, as potential sources of profit. The merchant class built industrialized nations by exploiting the labor and resources of the rest of the world. In capitalist eras, business leaders and corporate directors are depicted as heroes; wealth and power make them great.

Political rule is also determined by capitalists behind the scenes who buy and sell politicians and hold true power. All capitalist societies are in this condition now, as shown by the dependency of political leaders in most countries on "big money" to finance their election campaigns. Though constitutional democracy was a positive development in the merchant age, as practiced today it has largely become a tool of the financially powerful to control national economies.

Intellectuals and warriors are also bought by capitalists to do their bidding. Most scientific research that is funded benefits corporations or the military. The United States armed forces have approximately 800 formal military bases in 80 countries and go to war to protect US corporate interests (Slater 2018).

Today, the capitalist age is declining. Hunger, poverty and unemployment cause greater misery and affect more people than ever before. Decadence and degradation of the human spirit have become extreme. The gap between the rich and poor is greatly increasing. Money is acquired and hoarded by the rich, therefore circulating less in the economy. Most intellectuals and warriors are reduced to the economic condition of shudras. Fewer and fewer people benefit from capitalism. These are clear indicators of the extreme exploitation of the other classes by the capitalists.

Shudra Revolution and a New Cycle Begins

In the Social Cycle of Prout, due to increasing exploitation and eventual market failures, the common people—led by disgruntled intellectuals and warriors—will in time rise up in a popular revolt and take economic and social power into their own hands. This shudra revolution marks the end of the merchant era and the beginning of a new cycle.

Technically speaking, shudras should lead society in the wake of the overthrow of the vaeshyan order. However, this shudra period is, in effect, a very brief time of anarchy, lasting only as long as it takes the ksattriya leaders of the revolution to solidify their power. The workers' communist revolutions in Russia in 1917, followed by China, Yugoslavia, North Korea, Vietnam, Cuba, and other countries, qualify: vaeshya rule ended through shudra revolution, resulting in a new, ksattriya-led society.

The Social Cycle moves in constant rotation. Based on the traits of the different classes (varnas), we can detect distinct ages in the history of different societies. The social and administrative domination of one of the classes marks each age and shapes the main values and social psychology of the society. As a rule, at any given time, only one class is dominant in each society. The four ages of shudra, ksattriya, vipra, and vaeshya together make one complete spiral of the Social Cycle.

Within each spiral there is also a dialectical movement that accounts for the birth, maturity, and death of an age, leading to the birth, maturity, and death of the next age.

Spiritual Revolutionaries: *Sadvipras*

While Prout takes a macro view of class struggles, it also accepts that strong individuals have the ability to influence and offer hope to society. Prout sees that intellectually developed spiritual leaders called sadvipras (literally, those with subtle minds), will arise. Sadvipras are those who by virtue of their physical, mental, and spiritual efforts have developed the positive qualities of all classes combined. They also possess the moral force and courage to fight injustice and exploitation, and to protect the weak.

The qualities of a sadvipra include honesty, courage, dedication, and sacrificing spirit for humanity. They follow universal ethical principles. They are leaders devoted to the welfare of society. By personal example they inspire and guide society forward in a holistic and progressive way.

During his lifetime, Sarkar always spoke of this concept with the highest respect, saying that sadvipras embody the greatest ideals that one could aspire to hold. We can grasp that as society progresses, an ever-higher ethical standard will be expected of these spiritual revolutionaries.

Anyone can become a sadvipra by humbly learning the positive traits of all four classes and setting a personal example of self-discipline and service.

While Sarkar sees the rotation of the Social Cycle as inevitable, he believes these socio-spiritual visionaries who have struggled to rise above their class interests can smooth society's progress. Because they have risen above their class identity, they feel allegiance to everyone, not to any group or party or nation. They are open-minded, multicultural, and dedicated to justice for all. Without personal ambition, with a universal spiritual outlook, their thoughts are clear. Sarkar describes their role as one of working in the "nucleus" of the Social Cycle, helping each group to develop and lead society in turn. As soon as signs of social decay or exploitation appear, sadvipras will apply ample force by mobilizing the people to speed up the transition to the next varna, thereby decreasing periods of exploitation.

The magic of Sadvipra leadership was best captured by Lao Tzu: "A leader is best when people barely know she or he exists; when the work is done, the aim fulfilled, they will say: 'we did it ourselves.'"

Prout's model of sadvipra leadership seeks to harness the dynamic forces of humanity in a positive way. Prout uses the individual and collective potentials on all levels—physical, psychic, social and spiritual—and synthesizes them in an effort to create an ever more progressive and vibrant society.

Activist Tools: Becoming an Ideal Leader

Sarkar writes, "It becomes the prime duty of all people to make themselves and others sadvipras" (Sarkar 1967).

Sarkar stresses that there is a perennial conflict going on the world over between good and evil, light and darkness, virtue and vice. Humanity progresses through this conflict. Through this struggle for justice, through this churning, sadvipras are created.

However, spiritual revolutionaries also develop through another struggle, the inner one. Expanding one's mind continually through meditation and spiritual practice, must take place simultaneously with the struggle for social justice. Both are essential.

Sarkar revealed that in addition to one's conduct, morality and fighting spirit, one's universal outlook is also a way to judge whether a person is a sadvipra. "Due to their benevolent idealism and mental development they naturally look upon all with love and affection. They can never do any injustice in any particular era or to any particular individual" (Sarkar date unknown).

This is interesting, because conversely, a person's sentiment for a particular group would be a way to recognize that a person is not yet qualified to lead society. Some activists still hold an unconscious feeling of superiority of their nation, family, language, race or class. Some men and even some women distrust women leaders, and some women feel resentment against men because of this and so many wrongs committed.

The list of countries that have had a woman leader in modern times is relatively short. Women who have led countries have not stayed in power long, either. In the past fifty years, only 56 of the 146 nations (38 percent) studied by the World Economic Forum in 2014 and 2016 have had a female head of state for at least one year. In 31 of these countries, women have led for five years or less; in 10 nations, they have led for only a year (Geiger, Abigail & Kent 2017).

Why is there such a disparity in the number of women leaders? Part of the problem has to do with women being discriminated against if they have family and caregiving responsibilities and need family leave. The only two modern heads of state to give birth while in office were Prime Minister Benazir Bhutto of Pakistan in 1990, and Prime Minister Jacinda Ardern of New Zealand in 2018.

Women also face a double bind in that women who adopt masculine styles of leadership (directive and assertive behaviors) tend to be disliked and their ability to wield influence can be undermined. Yet women who embrace feminine stereotypes of cooperation and listening to all voices are sometimes thought to be too weak to be good leaders. Men who have assertive leadership styles, on the other hand, are respected and admired. Women also risk not getting a job or a promotion when they are too direct (Tepper, Brown & Hunt 1993).

Researchers at the University of Buffalo studied gender stereotypes over a 59-year-period with more than 19,000 participants and 136 studies from lab, business, and classroom settings. Emily Grijalva, Assistant Professor at the Buffalo School of Business Management, states:

> We found showing sensitivity and concern for others—stereotypically feminine traits—made someone less likely to be seen as a leader. However, it's those same characteristics that make

leaders effective. Thus, because of this unconscious bias against communal traits, organizations may unintentionally select the wrong people for leadership roles, choosing individuals who are loud and confident but lack the ability to support their followers' development and success (Biddle, Matthew August 7, 2018).

Even among activists, it is very easy to get attached to one's own plans. Yet if we refuse to listen to others and discuss other positions, then our rationality becomes of less concern than being "right."

All of these feelings have developed due to our background and our life's experiences. They are a natural result of what has happened, and yet they prevent us from "looking upon all with love and affection." Can we honestly say that we feel love and affection for every person we know? To strive for that highest spiritual outlook and to develop compassion for all is the personal goal of a spiritual revolutionary.

True leaders empower others to be great. They sincerely listen to the opinions of others, and they encourage and praise the accomplishments of others. Such leaders know that "who I am" does not depend on titles or positions. As loving parents are proud of the accomplishments of their children, these leaders show joy when others become great, too. Because economic democracy is about empowering people and communities, sadvipras are uniquely suited to facilitate this process.

The path of revolution is the most difficult path of all, and those who choose to walk this path will encounter greater and greater risks and challenges from many directions. Yet, the greatest enemies to be faced are one's own inner enemies and bondages: one's complexes, weaknesses, and fears. For example, many people are afraid of failure and of looking bad in front of others. Organizers will eventually find themselves faced with whatever it is they fear. The key is to confront these fears with courage and to overcome them.

The inner work of leaders is very important. As human beings, we all long for love, for approval, for certainty, for belonging. If we are not conscious of our own needs, then we tend to blame others for our unmet needs. Often we blame those who are around us.

The process of self-analysis is essential to inner progress: evaluating one's mistakes each day—indeed, each moment—and struggling to overcome each defect as it arises.

The downfall of many revolutionaries has been the desire for small comforts and security. The power of spiritual struggle, as embodied in the ancient science of Tantra Yoga, can help to overcome such desires. Rather than avoiding physical and psychic clashes, one needs to confront and embrace them for personal transformation and growth.

It is true that what we despise in others—the qualities that we hate—are actually within us. Every human being has the same basket of mental tendencies; we express them according to our individual nature. We tend to project what we dislike within ourselves onto others. We often see those we disagree with as enemies, and get into heated arguments and bitter conflicts. Projection is a trick the mind plays to avoid facing the enemies within.

There is a way to identify this. Think of someone with whom you have the greatest difference of opinion. This person may have done something wrong; you or others may have been hurt by their actions. But if you feel hatred, anger, or superiority toward this person, then that is a problem that you must face and overcome. While you may disagree with someone's actions, and while you should fight against immorality and injustice, you should not confuse a person's behavior with the person.

Sarkar counseled, "Even while dealing with persons of inimical nature, one must keep oneself free from hatred, anger, and vanity" (Sarkar 1975). The feeling of jealousy should be overcome by super-imposing the idea of friendliness toward that person. Hatred should be overcome by compassion and forgiveness, envy by praise and encouragement. This is, of course, not easy, but with constant effort each propensity can eventually be brought under firm control. It is a life-long practice of continual self-improvement. This effort is vital to the ethical basis of social responsibility.

Emotionally Intelligent Leaders

Effective leaders must develop what Daniel Goleman calls "emotional intelligence." This concept explains how some people may be brilliant intellectuals, with vast knowledge and skills, yet still be unable to understand or be sensitive to the impact they have on others. Those who lack emotional intelligence are unaware of how others feel. Ideal leaders are "visionary," "coaching," and "democratic," and rarely use the less effective "pace-setting" and "commanding" styles (Goleman, Boyatzis, and McKee 2002).

Most people connect more easily with others from the same cultural background. Yet in the struggle to change the world, we will have to live and work with people from other races, cultures and nations. Cultural clashes, translation difficulties, misunderstandings, disagreements about values, and different ways of seeing the world, are very real problems that leaders must face. Ideal leaders treat all people as their sisters and brothers, dealing fairly with everyone based on universal principles and individual merit.

Another key principle for all leaders is to set an example by individual conduct before asking others to do the same.

Some leaders, unfortunately, become arrogant. They believe that because their cause is great, they are also great. This is not necessarily so. Arrogant leaders lack sensitivity and care little for the feelings and values of others.

True leaders, instead of developing ego, develop humility. A leader who is humble gives joy and inspiration to others.

Insecure leaders feel threatened by the success of others. Some men feel threatened by the achievements of women and may even create obstacles in their paths to diminish their success. Insecure leaders, both men and women, often become fiercely competitive, viewing the success of another's project as a disgrace to them. Although healthy internal competition can inspire people to work harder, the spirit of coordinated cooperation is also needed.

Insecure leaders are also afraid of losing control. They are afraid to hear complaints or criticism, of doing things a new way, of challenge and change. They are afraid of failure. They do not realize that they can learn from every failure, that every unsuccessful effort is an opportunity for personal and collective growth. They fear that admitting a mistake and apologizing for it will mean a loss of face. On the contrary, an honest apology for an error along with a willingness to make up for it, whether it was done knowingly or not, heals hurt feelings and often increases one's esteem in the eyes of one's peers and the public.

Activities

Do as many as you can:
Do a survey of your family and friends. Ask each one, who was the worst leader they ever met, and who was the best? Ask them to explain why they feel that way about those people.

Try to contact a leader in your community whom you admire. Tell them that you admire them, that you're trying to become a leader, too, and that you'd like a few minutes of their time to ask their advice.

Make a short questionnaire for leaders and send it to at least a dozen leaders whom you admire. If only one out of ten take the time to respond, you're doing great!

Is there a leadership training course in your area? Check colleges, youth programs, and community centers. If you find one, learn as much as you about it and what they teach. Form your own opinion about the value of their program.

What are your shadows, inner enemies, complexes, weaknesses, and fears? How can you examine and confront them? Make a plan of what you need to work on to become an ideal leader, a spiritual revolutionary.

Further Readings

Friedman, Uri. 2016. "Why It's So Hard for a Woman to Become President of the United States." *The Atlantic,* November 12, 2016.

Logan, Ron. 2015. "Sadvipra Leadership." Prout Institute.

Covey, Stephen R. 1992. "Principle-Centered Leadership: An Executive Book Summary."

Turner, Caroline. "Obstacles for Women in Business—the Double Bind." *HuffPost,* December 6, 2017.

Further Viewings

Barstow, Cedar and Eva Fajardo. 2014. "Introduction to the Right Use of Power: The Heart of Ethics for the Helping Professional." Webinar by Addiction Professional. December 8, 2014. 1 hour 6 minutes.

Sandburg, Sheryl. 2010. "Why We Have Too Few Women Leaders." TEDWomen 2010. 14 minutes.

"Thoughts of PR Sarkar - Sadvipra Samaj." February 2, 2016. 8 minutes.

Westbrook, Adam. 2016. "The Simple Reason Things Always Go Wrong: the Peter Principle." April 20, 2016. 8 minutes.

Wiseman, Liz. 2017. "Leaders as Multipliers." November 28, 2017. 1 hour 2 minutes.

References

Beck, Randall and Jim Harter. 2015. "Managers Account for 70% of Variance in Employee Engagement." *Gallup Business Journal,* April 21, 2015.

Biddle, Matthew. "Many Don't See Women as Leaders at Work." Futurity- University at Buffalo. August 7, 2018.

Boal, Augusto. 2002. *Games for Actors and Non-actors.* New York: Routledge.

Epitropaki, Olga. 2012. "What Holds Women Back? Gender Barriers at Work."

Geiger, Abigail and Lauren Kent. 2017. "Number of Women Leaders Around the World has Grown But They're Still a Small Group." Pew Research Center. March 8, 2017.

Goleman, Daniel, Richard E. Boyatzis and Annie McKee. 2002. *Primal Leadership: Realizing the Power of Emotional Intelligence.* Cambridge, MA: Harvard Business School.

Hofherr, Justine. 2015. "Founders of Women's iLab Seek to Close the Gender Gap in Tech." March 8, 2015.

Patrick, Christopher, Don Fowles, and Robert Krueger. 2009. "Triarchic Conceptualization of Psychopathy: Developmental Origins of Disinhibition, Boldness, and Meanness." *Development and Psychopathology*. Cambridge University Press. 21 (3) (August): 913–938. doi:10.1017/S0954579409000492.

Peter, Laurence J. and Raymond Hull. 1969. *The Peter Principle: Why Things Always Go Wrong*. New York: William Morrow and Company.

Sarkar, P.R. "Dialectical Materialism and Democracy." (date unknown).

— 1967. "The Future of Civilization." *Cosmic Society*.

— 1975. *Ananda Marga Caryácarya Part 2*. "Pain⬚cadasha Shiila (The Fifteen Rules of Behaviour)." Calcutta: Ananda Marga Publications.

Slater, Alice. 2018. "The US Has Military Bases in 80 Countries. All of Them Must Close." *The Nation*, January 24, 2018.

Tepper, B. J., S. J. Brown, and M. D. Hunt. 1993. "Strength of Subordinates' Upward Influence Tactics and Gender Congruency Effects." *Journal of Applied Social Psychology*. Volume 23, Issue 22, November, pages 1903-1919.

Women's Ilab. 2017. "The Status of Women in Leadership Positions, According to an AAUW Study." *Huffington Post*. July 8, 2017.

MODULE 10: NEOHUMANISM

Check Your Understanding

At the end of this module, you should be able to explain the following concepts:

Why do the corporate media act like government and big business propaganda organs in the United States and Great Britain?

Why are stories of violence and sex so common on news programs?

What do ads sell?

What are sentiments, geo-sentiments, and socio-sentiments?

What is Neohumanism?

What are the limitations of humanism?

What is progress?

What is psychic exploitation?

What are culture, civilization, and pseudo-culture?

What is the true goal of education?

What is Neohumanist Education?

Why is critical study important?

What is privilege and who has it?

What are the two kinds of privilege?

The Social Reality: Media Lies

"All governments lie," said I.F. Stone, a radical American investigative journalist. Amy Goodman, host of the global news program *Democracy Now!* adds, "especially in times of war" (Peabody 2016). There is no overt government censorship in the United States and Great Britain, yet corporate media act very much like the propaganda organs of the government and big business.

Noam Chomsky and Edward S. Herman highlighted this in their famous book, *Manufacturing Consent*. They asserted that money and power are able to filter the news, to keep dissenters powerless and on the outside, and to allow powerful private interests to get their message across to the public. This is because:

- The main media outlets are very large corporations that are profit-driven.
- Advertising is the main source of their income.
- Media corporations rely on information that is fed to them by government and big business.
- Big business and government can generate a great amount of negative 'flak,' which is public criticism, angry letters, and complaints to sponsors about a news story they don't like. (Chomsky and Herman 1988).

An example of flak is the high-powered campaign to deny and dismiss the scientific consensus that climate change is a real danger and mostly caused by humans. This flak has resulted in the major U.S. media outlets falsely conveying the issue as an open debate in which many are skeptical.

How a poor family survives is not a news story, but whatever a very rich and famous celebrity does is global news. If a teacher, social worker, or other mentor throughout their lifetime empowers hundreds of young people to transform their lives, that is not a news story; yet if a madman picks up a gun and shoots five people at random, that is assured to be world news. To explain why, journalists have a saying: "If it bleeds, it leads." Because violence and sex are very attractive to people's baser instincts, when news shows compete for profit, it is much more profitable to have a lot of stories about violence and sex.

More than $545 billion was spent on advertising worldwide in 2016 (*Statista* 2018). The average United States citizen is exposed to 3,000 ads every single day. There are ads on buildings, sports stadiums, athletes' uniforms, billboards, bus stops, in doctor's offices, and many other places. Much of their effect is subconscious. Rance Crain, senior editor of *Advertising Age*, said, "Only eight percent of an ad's message is received by the conscious mind. The rest is worked and reworked deep within the recesses of the brain" (*AdAge* 1997).

For example, since the Coca-Cola Company began in 1886, it has convinced the majority of people in the world that its product—a clearly unhealthy sugar-laden beverage containing caffeine and phosphoric acid—will quench a thirst better than water, and bring happiness at the same time. Coke's most recent advertising slogans in media spots with good-looking young people have been "Open Happiness" and "Taste the Feeling." These happy images affect us subconsciously, so that the next time we're asked to choose something to drink, many people will unconsciously reach for a Coke (McQueen 2001).

Ads sell more than products. They sell values, they sell images, they sell concepts of love and sexuality, of success, and most important, of normalcy. They tell us who we are and who we should be. Much advertising tells us that the most important thing about men is to be strong, rich, and powerful, while the most important thing for women is their appearance.

Author and filmmaker Jean Kilbourne pioneered a shocking critique of how the advertising industry portrays women superficially, and objectifies them, which lowers women's self-esteem. Sexualized images of women are being used to sell nearly all kinds of goods. This degrades women, encourages abuse, and reinforces sexism (Jhally 2010).

Prout's Vision: Human Sentiments and Neohumanism

A sentiment is an emotional tendency to identify with things we like, with that which gives us pleasure. Sentiments are fueled by emotional energy and are a powerful motivational force. Yet our emotions by themselves tend to be blind and unreliable guides to action.

It is common to feel allegiance to one's family and close circle of friends. In many parts of the world, membership in a clan, tribe or community is vital. Most people also regard themselves to be members or citizens of a certain region or nation, sometimes believing that their country is somehow better and more important than any other. P.R. Sarkar refers to this type of patriotism or nationalism as 'geo-sentiment.' Believing that one's nation is superior to others is expressed negatively in the slogan "My country, right or wrong!" and in discrimination against foreigners. It was this sentiment that gave the emotional justification for colonialism and imperialism.

Identifying more with one's own race, religion, class or gender, to the exclusion of other groups, is known as 'socio-sentiment.' Both geo-sentiment and socio-sentiment have led to countless tragic conflicts and wars that are, in his words, "the black spot of human character" (Sarkar 1981, 91). Politicians who exploit these sentiments to gain popularity may become quite powerful, but they can lead their entire community or nation to ruin.

"Neohumanism" is a term coined by Sarkar, and explained at length in his book, *The Liberation of Intellect: Neohumanism*. It expresses the process of expanding one's sentiment or allegiance outward from mere self-interest to one of empathy and identification with an ever-larger share of humanity and the universe.

Enlightened education that develops the rational, questioning mind can be an antidote to limiting sentiments and prejudices. When the raw, powerful energy of emotion is harnessed and guided by critical thinking, conscience, and benevolence, it transforms into one of the strongest forces of the universe.

If education expands our sense of identity to include all humanity, we will inevitably feel pain at the suffering of others, wherever they may be. This in turn inspires us to commit ourselves to social justice and service.

Why Neohumanism? The philosophy of humanism originated in Europe during the Renaissance in reaction to the illogical dogmas, sexual abuse, and dominance of the Catholic Church. In that era, powerful clergy demanded blind faith and total obedience. Later, during the Age of Enlightenment, many Western humanists rejected the idea of a transcendent God outside of human experience. Instead they relied on logic, scientific inquiry, and reason, trusting only what could be observed and measured. This freed them from church rule, but it led to a new dogma of material physics and "scientific" materialism as the sole power to decide all truth and fact.

The rejection of God forced humanists to search deeply for the personal and political meaning of such concepts as "liberty, equality, and fraternity," a slogan of the French Revolution. Humanists struggled to find a more natural and rational morality. Soon, however, they ran into the problem of relative morals. Liberty from what? Equality in relation to what? Good and evil seemed to depend on who was judging.

Within such a relative framework, the purpose of life is not always clear. This can leave the humanist in a spiritual vacuum, without transcendent values or direction—adrift on a sea of shifting, confusing ideas.

Humanism has other limitations. When tied to countries, as in the case of the United Nations, its followers may be plagued by political differences and jealousies. If it is based on the belief that there is nothing greater than the human ego, that there is no higher consciousness within us, humanists can become cynical and materialistic.

The philosophy of humanism may also lead a person to neglect other species, to consider them inferior and to exploit them for profit. Neohumanism urges us to rise above this limitation by including all of life in our definition of what is real, important, and deserving of respect. Although human beings are the most evolved species on this planet, other animals have awareness and feelings, too. Our actions and conduct should show love and respect toward all beings and inanimate objects in the universe.

Thus, an outlook based on universalism and Neohumanism is one that recognizes the spiritual family of humanity, a family that transcends nations and is rooted in spiritual ecology. Neohumanism is an expansive concept promoting physical welfare and security, mental learning, spiritual growth, and fulfillment. Neohumanism frees us from narrow sentiments and doctrines, as well as creating a shared sense of compassion. Viewing all human beings and the rest of this universe as the children of one Supreme Consciousness, one feels that the world's sorrow is his or her own sorrow, and the world's happiness is his or her own happiness.

A New Definition of Progress

Every being in this universe is moving—even inanimate objects vibrate on the atomic level. However, movement only has meaning or purpose when it is directed toward a goal. Prout defines social progress as movement directed toward the goal of well-being for all, from the first expression of moral consciousness to the formation of universal Neohumanism.

Prout uses the analogy of humanity as a family, or a group of people traveling on a pilgrimage, who stop if any member of their group is injured or falls sick. The American poet, Carl Sandburg, wrote:

There is only one man, and his name is all men.
There is only one woman, and her name is all women.
There is only one child, and its name is all children (Sandburg 1967).

Human society should facilitate the collective movement and growth of everyone. This requires a collective consciousness and social connection or solidarity.

Progress is commonly thought to mean increases in material comfort, or advances in technology. Prout, however, asserts that no true progress is ever really possible in the physical realm. This is because all physical things eventually decay, and any physical strength we build up will, in the end, be lost by accident, illness, or old age. Physical inventions, while making our lives easier and more comfortable, also create problems, dangers, and side effects. In the past, for example, when people walked or rode animal carts, few suffered critical injuries in accidents—now nearly 1.25 million people die in road crashes each year, and 20 to 50 million are injured or disabled (ASIRT 2018).

It is also clear that increases in knowledge, communication, and mental activity are not always truly progressive and helpful to one's deeper well-being. Stress, anxiety, depression, and mental disease are much more common among educated, urban populations in industrialized societies than among less educated rural people. It is also true that what we learn can be forgotten.

Prout accepts that only those physical actions and mental expressions that promote progress toward the state of infinite well-being are truly progressive. For example, assuring all the right to work and earn the basic necessities of life ensures collective peace of mind. When people no longer have to worry about how they will provide food, clothing, housing, education, and medical care for their families, they will be free to develop their higher mental and spiritual qualities.

Psychic Exploitation

When P.R. Sarkar first introduced Prout in 1959, there was a great need for cultural recovery following the colonial rule of India and the rest of the so-called Third World. Besides political and economic exploitation, the cultural identity of the people had been harmed. Sarkar pointed out the need to reclaim local traditions, knowledge, memory, and identity.

Sarkar explained how psychic exploitation takes place in three ways. First, in both rich and poor countries, public education is neglected. Little money is allotted to public schools, and most elites send their children to costly private schools. Because of lack of proper funding, public schools cannot attract the most qualified people to teach, and cannot afford other curricular and extra-curricular programs that stimulate and enrich the lives of the students. This neglect causes academic standards to fall, teachers and students to lose their spirit, and rising levels of school dropouts.

Secondly, there is a lack of development of social and economic awareness, a factor which maintains the cycle of exploitation. The great Brazilian educator Paulo Freire condemned this lack of critical awareness:

> Fundamentally, I think that one of the things that is lacking in us in the learning experience, in both teachers and students, is an experience of critical reflection about our presence in the world. What is generally emphasized in most schools is the transfer of content, transferring information of biology, geography, history, and mathematics that minimizes the importance of your presence in the world (Maheshvarananda 2006).

Freire revolutionized the teaching of literacy through dialogue, recognizing and respecting the knowledge that poor people already have. He also helped them to question the reasons for their poverty in a process that he called "conscientization."

A third type of psychic exploitation is to instill fear and inferiority complexes in people in order to keep them passive. For example, the capitalist media promotes the idea that anyone can become rich. It can be logically inferred, therefore, by anyone who is not rich, that it is somehow their fault that they are not. Unemployed people often suffer depression, a low self-esteem, and sometimes a bitterness and anger at society which can tragically explode in violent acts of crime.

The dominant message in capitalism is self-centered and competitive: "First get an education; then get a job; make as much money as you can; and buy as much as you can." The media rarely convey a message of duty toward others in our human family. Many governments and private corporations advertise lotteries and gambling casinos to poor people, encouraging them to dream of getting rich. This selfish, materialistic attitude is expressed as, "I win, you lose," or more correctly, "I win, and it doesn't matter to me what happens to anyone else." This selfish outlook destroys human relations, communities, and the planet itself.

Culture, Civilization and Pseudo-Culture

The social life of people depends on their culture and civilization. Prout defines culture as a variety of human expressions, including traditions, customs, art, language, dress, and diet. In every community of the world, culture has matured naturally along with the development of the human intellect.

Civilization, on the other hand, pertains to the level of humanity and rationality present in a culture. Some traditional cultures have been plagued with superstitions, intolerance, and violence. Other societies may represent a high degree of culture, but if they allow their people to discriminate, exploit, or claim superiority, Prout would regard them as uncivilized.

Prout's universal outlook recognizes unity in human diversity. It accepts that human culture is really one, with many local variations that enhance the beauty of humanity. The basic nature of the human mind is the same everywhere, but our tendencies are expressed in various ways and amounts in different places. In order for true unity to develop, we must honor this diversity while recognizing our inherent oneness.

Throughout history, some cultures have tried to destroy others. In the past, imperialists used superior weapons to invade and conquer other lands. They told the defeated people, "Your culture is primitive; your religion is defective; your language is unsophisticated." The invaders used violence and imposed an inferiority complex to break the people's will to resist.

When colonialism gradually collapsed after the Second World War, capitalists invented clever techniques to continue exploiting the newly independent countries. One of their most powerful tricks has been to impose pseudo-culture.

Pseudo-culture means that which is fake, imposed, and which does not uplift a people. It is a construct of ideas and products that weaken the social outlook of a people and prepare them to be exploited. Pseudo-culture offers to make life more pleasant than it was under their own culture, but in fact, it weakens people mentally and spiritually and lowers their will to resist.

Many of the television programs broadcast around the world promote a U.S. consumer pseudo-culture. This can have a damaging effect on one's personality. Ads portray a life that seems to be more pleasurable than one's real life. Such ads can make people want to be rich and white—to enjoy the flashy clothes, cars, and houses that almost everyone in Hollywood TV shows and films seems to have. Most children around the world see their parents struggling, living with much less income and fewer material goods, and so they start to feel that they are backward and deprived of the good life. If children want to be someone else, it means they don't want to be themselves. Even young children begin to develop a low self-image and inferiority complex because of pseudo-culture.

The corporate-owned mass media continually promote the desire to get rich quick; they do not broadcast revolutionary music, theater or news. Pseudo-culture paralyzes people and breaks their will to fight exploitation. It is very negative and divisive, confusing people as to who the real enemy is and weakening their courage to unite and resist.

An Educational Revolution

Prout recognizes that teaching is one of the most important professions. Education, both formal and informal, should be society's highest priority. It should be available to all free of charge, funded by the government. However community school systems and universities, in collaboration with teachers and parents, should run the schools, free from political control.

Prout proposes that the media should be taken from the control of the capitalists and run by cooperatives of journalists, artists and educators. These co-ops would try to promote popular education for all ages. It should be inspiring, with uplifting culture, cardinal human values and universalism.

The goal of education should be liberation, to free people from mental bondages and limitations and to promote solidarity. Teaching cardinal human values is very important, rousing in the students a sense of caring for the welfare of others. Our education should begin with mutual respect for different outlooks and ideas. It will strive to make students aware and awaken consciousness.

The Neohumanist system of education is based on "the practice of love for all creation including plants, animals, and the inanimate world" as propounded by Prabhat Ranjan Sarkar. It includes a harmonious blending of Eastern introversial philosophy and Western extroversial science. The focus of Neohumanist Education is on physical, mental, and spiritual self-development, human values, universal love, and applied learning. Personal growth includes areas such as morality, integrity, self-confidence, self-discipline, and cooperation.

Worldwide, Neohumanist Education is practiced in a network of schools and institutes that span over fifty countries with hundreds of kindergartens, primary schools, high schools, colleges, and children's homes. This global education network is called *Gurukula*, which means an institution that helps students dispel the darkness of the mind and leads to total emancipation of each person and of society at large. The Gurukula network of Neohumanist schools and institutes aims to hasten the advent of a society in which there is love, peace, understanding, inspiration, justice, and health for all beings.

At Gurukula, all aspects of the human personality are developed, using an integrated curriculum that empowers the student to know him or herself, and to use this knowledge in order to serve society. The Gurukula curriculum focuses on intellectual ability, but also includes the development of intuition, aesthetics, and an ecological viewpoint. The main campus for Ananda Marga Gurukula is in Anandanagar, West Bengal, India, where an educational township on a 550-square-kilometer rural campus is being built. Current projects include Composite Medical Services, Veterinary Institute, Acupuncture Clinic, Music College, Naturopathy Institute, and Teacher Training College.

Neohumanist institutions, which include educational and research institutes, academies, conference centers, colleges, and universities, have started in the United States (Asheville, NC), Sweden (Ydrefors), Singapore, Argentina, Taiwan, and Italy. These offer adult courses in an array of subjects aimed at liberating the intellect and promoting individual and collective welfare.

Activist Tools: Critical Thinking and Unpacking Privilege

Critical Thinking: Both advertisements and political propaganda try to manipulate us, often with an arrogant disdain toward the people's intelligence. In his book, *The Liberation of Intellect: Neohumanism*, P.R. Sarkar prescribes three stages to overcome lies and manipulation. The first stage is critical study. He defines study as "intensive intellectual analysis." To prevent manipulation, we need to study and carefully analyze.

Study means to gather information from all angles. We should not only rely on books and research, we should talk with people and seek direct experiences to come to a more balanced view about the world and its people.

In the case of advertising, we could study why some ads appeal so strongly to our emotions. Happy actors in stunning scenery with soothing music creates a pleasant feeling in us. If those good-looking actors are smoking cigarettes, then it will cause many people to link smoking with happiness. Cigarette ads convinced many people, including young children, to begin smoking, and to become addicted to tobacco. A coalition of anti-tobacco groups were able to get these ads banned in most countries.

One potential defect in study is due to ignorance, when we unknowingly pass on incorrect information, unaware that we are spreading "fake news." Another possible defect is due to changes in time, when we unknowingly pass on knowledge that was once true, but is no longer true.

After carefully studying an issue, the second stage to overcome lies and manipulation is to consider the pros and cons of both sides of an issue. If the positive side is predominant, we will give that side our vote. If the negative aspect is predominant, we will decide against the issue.

In the third stage, we need to decide whether this will contribute to the welfare of all. If we develop a firm rationalistic mentality, no one will be able to deceive us by false sentiments, and we will gain inner strength and resolution (Sarkar, 1982).

Unpacking Privilege: In her article, "White Privilege and Male Privilege," Peggy McIntosh defines privilege as "unearned power conferred systematically" (McIntosh 1988). Privilege is hard to see for those who were born with access to power and resources. It is very visible for those to whom privilege was not granted. For those who have privilege based on race, gender, class, physical ability, sexual orientation, or age, it is just normal.

There are two kinds of privilege. The first kind includes things of value that all people *should have*, such as feeling safe in public spaces or working in a place where they feel they belong and are valued for what they can contribute. Tragically, many women and other oppressed peoples around the world face discrimination, invisible barriers, and sometimes violence to prevent them from becoming equals with the privileged classes. The goal of Prout is to create a global society where everyone is guaranteed the minimum requirements, where everyone feels safe from violence, and where everyone has equal opportunities in educational and professional training, as well as a chance to fully develop their artistic and spiritual potential.

The second kind of privilege goes a step further by giving one group power over another. The common practice of men speaking more than women in conversations, for example, is based on a cultural assumption, often unconscious, that men are more intelligent than women. A husband who appears in any way subordinate to his wife is often labeled "henpecked" or worse; the English language contains no specific insulting terms for a woman who is under the control of her husband.

Here are just a few other examples of privilege:

- In the United States, statistics show that racial minorities are more likely than white Americans to be arrested. Once arrested, they are more likely to be convicted, and once convicted, they are more likely to face stiff sentences. The best national evidence on drug use shows that African Americans and whites use illegal drugs at about the same rate. Yet African Americans are about five times as likely to go to prison for drug possession as whites (The Sentencing Project 2013).
- In most countries, there is a disproportionately high number of white males in government and the ruling circles of corporations and universities.
- Those in privileged groups have an easier time getting a loan, or renting or buying a house wherever they want. They have greater access to quality education and health care.
- Those who are privileged can count on the fact that their nation's history books will include their experience of history. Indigenous people and women, on the other hand, know that their children will not learn in school about their people, except in mostly stereotypical accounts. Traditionally, history books have not included women who have distinguished themselves, nor has the history of women been taught in schools. From the first recorded law in 2400-2300 BC, which says that when a woman speaks out of turn she will be smacked by a brick, there has been a conspiracy to silence women (Heing 2015).
- Those in privileged groups generally assume that when they go out in public, they won't be challenged and asked to explain what they're doing, or physically attacked because of their race, gender, or sexual orientation.
- Those in privileged groups can reasonably expect that if they work hard and "play by the rules," they'll get what they deserve. They can succeed without other people being surprised. If they fail, they will be given a second chance and allowed to treat their failure as a learning experience.

Different groups of people in different countries have privilege. In all the European countries, Australia, New Zealand, Canada, and the United States, the white race has privilege. Throughout Latin America, the white descendants of Europeans have privilege.

In India, the Brahmin high caste dominates the Hindu religion, Indian politics, and the Indian economy. Discrimination against lower castes is illegal under Article 15 of the Indian Constitution, but the caste system is still very much alive. About half the population is classified as lower caste. More than 47,000 crimes against lower castes were reported in 2016 alone (Couderé 2016). A 2014 survey by the Indian National Council of Applied Economic Research of 42,000 households found that almost one-third of those who were upper caste would not admit a person from the Dalit, Bahujan, or Adivasi communities (the so-called untouchable or casteless) into their kitchen or to use their utensils. Only five percent of the women surveyed had married someone from another caste. At election time, most Indians vote for politicians based on their caste (Chishti 2014).

Those who are privileged think of themselves as just people, not part of any special group; however, others may see them in this way. So, what should people of privilege do to make the world a better place in which all of us can live?

To challenge systems of privilege, we must explore and talk about them. This is usually uncomfortable for those in privileged groups. McIntosh writes that "the pressure to avoid [talking about privilege] is great, for in facing it I must give up the myth of meritocracy," that is, the idea that those with wealth and power earned it purely by their hard work, talent, and superior intelligence (McIntosh, 1988).

Those who are not reaping the unearned benefits of privilege must challenge those who wield the power of their privilege either consciously or unconsciously. Confronting privilege is often difficult and unpleasant, and sometimes, even dangerous. In fact, though, to insist on equal treatment as a woman, a person of color, an immigrant, or as a member of any oppressed group, is important. Speaking truth to power is absolutely essential in making any significant change in the power structure, whether it be the patriarchy or the capitalist system, both of which are inexorably linked.

Activities

Do as many as you can:

Count the stories on a TV news show. How many of them are about violence or sex?

Find out whether there is an anti-racism organization or campaign in your community. If so, visit them and ask what their challenges and successes have been.

Find out whether there is an anti-sexism organization or campaign in your community. If so, visit them and ask what their challenges and successes have been.

Buy or borrow a popular magazine in your country. Count all the people pictured in all the advertisements. How many of them represent each race that lives in your country? Are the proportions the same as in the general population? Do the same with TV, counting all the people in the commercials. Are any of them overweight? Do any of them have disabilities? Do any of them represent different cultures?

Start a discussion about privilege.

Further Readings

Ananda Devapriya, Didi. 2018. "Sentiment, Rationality and Intuition in Neohumanism." *Gurukula Network*, Issue 46, July.

Jacobson, Eric. 2014. "What is Neohumanism, and What is Neohumanist Education?" *Gurukula Network*, Issue 38.

Kendall, Francis. 2002. "Understanding White Privilege." 11 pages.

Logan, Ron. 2015. "Neohumanism: The Only Open Road into the Future." Prout Institute.

McIntosh, Peggy. 1988. "White Privilege and Male Privilege: A Personal Account of Coming to See Correspondences Through Work in Women's Studies."

Okun, Tema. 2001. "White Supremacy Culture." Changework.

Further Viewings

Abhidevananda Avadhuta. 2012. "Neohumanism (Section 1 of 4)." October 15, 2012. 8 minutes.

Adichie, Chimamanda Ngozi. 2011. "We Should All be Feminists." TEDXEuston. 2011. 29 minutes.

Alister, Paul Narada. 2009. "Neo Humanist Education." December 8, 2009. 7 minutes.

Johnson, Allan. 2015. "Power, Privilege and Difference with Dr. Allan Johnson." March 25, 2015. 1 hour.

Peabody, Fred, Peter Raymont, Jeff Cohen, and John Westhauser, directors. 2016. "All Governments Lie - Truth, Deception, and the Spirit of I.F. Stone." Documentary. 1 hour 32 minutes.

Woodland, Dane. 2017. "How Male Privilege Made Me a Feminist." TEDxYouth@StJohns. December 8, 2017. 8 minutes.

References

AdAge. 1997. "Viewpoint: Who Knows What Ads Lurk in the Hearts of Consumers? The Inner Mind Knows." June 9, 1997.

Association for Safe International Road Travel. 2018. "Annual Global Road Crash Statistics."

Chishti, Seema. 2014. "Biggest Caste Survey: One in Four Indians Admit to Practising Untouchability." *The Indian Express*, November 29, 2014.

Coudéré, Hanne. 2016. India: "Violence Against Dalits on the Rise." *The Diplomat*, May 19, 2016.

Herman, Edward and Noam Chomsky. 1988. *Manufacturing Consent: The Political Economy of the Mass Media.* New York: Pantheon Books.

Jhally, Sut, dir. 2010. "Killing Us Softly 4: Advertising's Image of Women" documentary.

Maheshvarananda, Dada. 2006. "Conversation with Paulo Freire, Educator of the Oppressed," in Sohail Inayatullah, Marcus Bussey, and Ivana Milojević, eds. *Neohumanist Educational Futures: Liberating the Pedagogical Intellect.* Taipei: Tamkang University.

McIntosh, Peggy. 1988. "White Privilege and Male Privilege: A Personal Account of Coming to See Correspondences Through Work in Women's Studies."

McQueen, Humphrey. 2001. *The Essence of Capitalism: How We can Learn Everything About Modern Companies and the Way the Global Economy is Run by International Corporations from the Biggest Soft Drinks Maker in the World.* London: Profile Books Ltd.

Peabody, Fred, Peter Raymont, Jeff Cohen, and John Westhauser, dir. 2016. All Governments Lie: Truth, Deception, and the Spirit of I.F. Stone. Documentary.

Sandburg, Carl. 1967. "Timesweep," in *Honey and Salt.* Boston: Houghton Mifflin Harcourt.

Sarkar, P.R. 1981. *Thoughts of P.R. Sarkar.* Calcutta: Ananda Marga Publications.

— 1982. "Awakened Conscience (Discourse 9)" in *The Liberation of Intellect: Neohumanism.* Kolkata: Ananda Marga Publications.

Statista. 2018. "Global Advertising Spending from 2014 to 2021 (in Billion U.S. Dollars)."

The Sentencing Project. 2013. "Report to the United Nations Human Rights Committee Regarding Racial Disparities in the United States Criminal Justice System." August 2013.

Course Evaluation

Tools to Change the World
Study Guide Based on the Progressive Utilization Theory (Prout) – Level 1
Please help us improve this course by filling out this evaluation at https://prout.info/course-evaluation/. Or mail it to us at Dada Maheshvarananda, 6 Breyerton Court, Asheville, NC 28804, USA. Thank you for your participation.

Your Experience
1) Where did you take or read this course? Please list city, state or province, and country
_____

2) How did you hear about this? From a friend ___ a flyer ___ TV, radio, or newspaper ___ the Internet (which site?) _____ other (please specify) _____

3) Did you read or take this course alone? Yes/No

4) How many hours on average did you spend doing readings, viewings and activities for each module? _____

5) Did the course inspire you to do something? Yes/No. If Yes, what? _____

6) Do you plan to repeat this course? Yes/No and why? _____

7) Would you be interested to take Level 2 of "Tools to Change the World" when it is ready? Yes/No

Course Content: 5= excellent, 4=good, 3=average, 2= below average, and 1= needs a lot of improvement.

	5	4	3	2	1
8) How clear was the manual?					
9) How useful were the content and tools for you?					
10) How did the course develop your ability to think critically about the world?					
11) How useful did you find the Activities?					
12) How useful did you find the Further Readings and Viewings?					
13) How well did the course give you confidence to talk to people you meet about these subjects?					

Group Process: Answer these questions only if you took the course with others.
14) How many other people started the course with you? ___
15) How many of those people continued until the end? ___
16) How many sessions did you attend? _____
17) Was the place or places you met conducive for the meeting? Y/N
18) How long were your meetings? ____

19) Did you feel that the length of time was right? Y/N If no, what would have been a better length?

_____

	5	4	3	2	1
20) How much did you feel challenged and inspired by the other participants?					
21) How focused were most of the discussions?					
22) How well did the meetings start on time?					
23) How well did the rotation of facilitation work?					
24) How well did you do when you were facilitator?					
25) How well did the opening Excitement Sharing go?					
26) How well did the Social Reality Discussions go?					
27) How well did the Cooperative Games go?					
28) How well did the presentations of Prout's Vision go?					
29) How well did the Activist Tools Training go?					
30) How democratic were discussions, with everyone getting a chance to speak and no one dominating?					
31) How satisfied were you with your effort in this course?					

4. Open-Ended Questions

32) What do you feel were the strengths of this course?

33) How could this course be improved?

34) Would you recommend this course to others? If so, what advice would you give to another person who is considering taking this course?

INDEX

ABOUT THE AUTHORS

Dada Maheshvarananda: Born in 1953 in Philadelphia, USA, during college he was active in the protests against the Vietnam War. In 1978 he traveled to India and Nepal where he became a yogic monk and studied Prout under its founder, Prabhat Ranjan Sarkar. He has taught meditation and organized for social justice for four decades in Southeast Asia, Europe, and South America. He is the author of six books, including *After Capitalism: Economic Democracy in Action* (InnerWorld, 2013) and *Cooperative Games for a Cooperative World: Facilitating Trust, Communication and Spiritual Connection* (InnerWorld, 2017). His books have been published in ten languages. He has given hundreds of seminars and workshops around the world at international conferences, universities, high schools, cooperatives, yoga centers and prisons about social activism and spiritual transformation. He can be reached at maheshvarananda@prout-global.org.

Mirra Price grew up in Indiana where she attended college in the mid-1960s, and organized against the Vietnam War. Leaving the male dominated anti-war movement in 1969, she helped start the Women's Liberation Movement, to advocate for the equality of women. During college, she was part of a work collective which managed a Prout food co-op. While teaching English on the Dineh (Navajo) Reservation, as a Proutist, she joined with Dineh Resistors to Forced Relocation in their struggle to stay on their land and preserve their native culture. She has two masters' degrees in education, one in bi-lingual education from Northern Arizona University and one from Harvard in educational media. She has edited several alternative newsletters, has published poetry, short stories, articles, and blogs. As editor of the North American Women Proutists' Rising Sun newsletter (2011-2018), she encouraged women to tell their stories, and has worked to make space for the voices of women in Prout and the social justice movement. She has given many talks and workshops at retreats, conferences, and schools on social justice, women's equality, and eco-feminism. Believing in the intersectionality of social movements, she networks with members of the #MeToo, Women's March, Black Lives Matter, Poor Peoples' Campaign, #NeverAgain youth, Sanctuary, Anti-Pipeline, and other movements whose members advocate for the rights of all oppressed peoples. She is currently a free-lance copy-editor at mirraedits.com.

Notes

Notes

Notes